MANAGING LIBRARY IN ELECTRONIC ERA:
Principles and Practice

MANAGING LIBRARY IN ELECTRONIC ERA:
Principles and Practice

Editors
Surendra Sethy
Rabindra Kumar Mahapatra

Ess Ess Publications
New Delhi

MANAGING LIBRARY IN ELECTRONIC ERA: Principles and Practice

ISBN: 978-81-933597-5-4

First Published 2017

Published by:
Ess Ess Publications
4831/24, Ansari Road,
Darya Ganj,
New Delhi-110 002.
INDIA
Phones: 23260807, 41563444
Fax: 41563334
E-mail: info@essessreference.com
www.essessreference.com

Cover Design by *Patch Creative Unit*

Printed and bound in India at Salasar Imaging Systems.

Contents

Foreword

With the advent of computerization, digitization of records, and enhanced information management and retrieval, the library and information science has experienced dramatic growth and change. It has now emerged as a professional field with challenging prospects.

The book entitled, "Managing Library in Electronic Era: Principles and Practices" could not have come at a better time than now, given the global nature of the Library and Information Science (LIS) profession. In particular, it is important for the developing nations to understand the practice of LIS professions in their environments so as to adapt to the best practices being followed globally. It is important to note that comprehensive knowledge about digitation and electronic library management is a "sine qua non" for the students and professionals of Library and Information Science discipline.

This book provides a valuable window on information assurance and essential topics on management of library electronically. The topics in the book covers a wide range of areas within the discipline, which include: digital preservation of data, digital preservation policy, exploration of e-resources for library, cloud technology and its application library, quality management practices in academic library, online courses having relevance to library science, role of leadership in digital environment etc.

With more than 50 percent of today's gross national product related to the management of information, the book shall be useful for the undergraduate and post-graduate level students and working professionals.

I must congratulate Dr. Surendra Sethy and Dr. R.K. Mahapatra, Editors of the book, for being able to obtain review articles from distinguished authors, on contemporary issues on management of library electronically.

This gives me immense pleasure to recommend this book to all stakeholders involved in library and information practices. I consider this book to be an useful addition to the literature of library and information science.

February 23, 2017

Prof. Pradip C Deka
Vice Chancellor
Sir Padampat Singhania University
Udaipur, Rajasthan

Preface

For the foreseeable future Library and Information Science and information technology is likely to be one of the most potent growth areas in our field. Indeed it is now widely recognized that long-term economic prosperity will crucially depend upon people's success in developing, mastering, exploiting and marketing library and information systems.

Although the argument for the rapid development and introduction of information technology (IT) with Library and Information Science into the many aspects of our everyday existence is extremely strong, unfortunately it remains the case that at present the technology is being used effectively by only a small proportion of the people who could benefit from it. As the chapters in this book illustrate examples of modern trends to be applied in Library and Information Science as a result of IT application and implementation in our field is legion.

The message of the volume is clear. Previous attempts to apply and implement IT into the field of Library and Information Science have remained mostly unsuccessful because the approach was not holistic. Unless the new technologies are designed and introduced with an appreciation of the needs and reactions of those who will use and be affected by them, the chances that they will operate effectively are slight.

It is the people who have to operate systems built around the new technologies, and who have to interact with them to make them function. It is the people who have to accept the systems and their intrusion into work and home. It is the people who are often called on to adapt their habits to the dictates of the system, and who often cannot do so. In short, the application of knowledge about human behaviour, actions, thoughts, feelings, education, etc., has often been insufficient or missing. This is both unfortunate and unnecessary, for sophisticated behavioral models and methods are now available. As the chapters in this volume indicate, psychological approaches have much to offer both in predicting and understanding users' potential needs and problems, and in developing new approaches to the crucial issues of technological design and management.

The editors would like to place on record the excellent help rendered by each one of the author for their valued contributions. Special thanks to Dr. K. Nazeer Badhusha for all along support in this endeavor. Thanks are also due to M/S Ess Ess Publications, New Delhi for accepting the request and publishing this volume.

We wish to express our sincere gratitude to Mr. Ashok Ghosh, President and Mrs. Rinu Ghosh, Vice President of Sir Padampat Singhania Unviersity (SPSU), Udaipur, Rajasthan. We also very much thankful to Prof. (Dr.) P. C. Deka, Vice Chancellor, SPSU, Udaipur for his invaluable suggestions.

The final tribute and greatest appreciation, however, is reserved for my (Dr. Surendra Sethy) father (Late) Trinath Sethy and mother Smt. Kuntala Devi, wife Oliva and daughter Riddhivi for their cooperation & constant support.

Despite utmost care, errors might have crept in and the authors will be thankful if these are brought to their knowledge. Any suggestion for the improvement of this book will be thankfully acknowledged.

Surendra Sethy

Rabindra Kumar Mahapatra

1

Emerging Mobile Technology and Mobile Users in Academic Libraries

Basanta Kumar Das*
Sanjay Kumar Karn**

ABSTRACT

Information and Communication Technologies (ICTs) have changed the way of people's to access and communicate information. Modern mobile devices which have powerful features for which are transforming access to information. In the information transfer age mobile devices such as smart phones become 'major information devices' for users. Therefore, Libraries will want to have a significant presence in offering content and reference services that are suitable for this medium of communication. Users want easy and instant access to relevant information, aspiring from Library and Information Science (LIS) professionals to think out of the box for meeting their information needs. With handheld mobile or portable devices such as smart (cell) phones, laptops,

* Counsellor & Executive Asst., IGNOU Regional Centre, Ranchi-834022, Jharkhand, India.

* Asst. University Librarian & I/C, Central Library, Ranchi University, Morabadi

iPods etc., the paper hints at the application of instant messaging (IM), social media platforms such as Skype, OoVoo etc., Short Message Service (SMS), and blogs, among others, as usable devices in reference information service.

Mobile devices are the widely used scientific gadgets among all available in the current society. Keeping mobile phone is a kind of necessity today after food, shelter, dress. People of every age group are frequently using mobile phones not for conversation only but for acquiring their required piece of information from the global village i.e. Internet. Users can access the treasure of knowledge available on WWW whenever they want. The number of mobile phone users increased many fold with the increase in mobile applications from telephonic conversation to multimedia and internet.

Keywords : ICT, SMS, LIS, Smart Phones, MMS, Video Calling

INTRODUCTION

Advancements in Information communication technology have contributed in availability of various useful gadgets for each and every aspect of human life in 21st century. In the present age, it's difficult to manage life without these gadgets after food, shelter and home. More and more people are using devices such as mobile phones to seek information, not just to communicate but for acquiring global knowledge from news to food. Information and communication technology provided faster access to information and it is challenging for the libraries to rethink and remodel their new services adopting the technological changes. The mobile revolution is very much upon us. People are moving rapidly from ordinary cell phones to smart phones, in both developed and developing countries like India. Mobile phones were basically meant for only to reduce the time lag and create wireless communication among distance living people. Mobile phones are become more popular because of the additional features like, camera, recorder, music player, radio, SMS, MMS sending facility and many application oriented app. Moreover the new phones with additional facility of memory cards have turned it into information storing and disseminating device. And now smart phones with the facility of Internet access on mobile has made it an information retrieval device. In the past decades some technological changes have appeared gradually and their impact on higher education has been incremental. Introduction of web browsers have had a major and some would say revolutionary, impact on education as well as the broader society. Which will it be for mobile devices? Will their impact be gradual and incremental or sudden and revolutionary? There is a case for both points of view. Since individuals have been using devices such as laptops and mobile phones for decades, on might argue that the impact of the use of mobile devices on peoples' behavior in general and on higher education in particular has been relatively gradual. On the other hand, as devices with compelling new features emerge and wireless connectivity is almost ubiquitously available, we may be on the verge of a revolutionary phase of mobile device impact on higher education and libraries. Apart from approach of libraries about using mobile phone in library environment, because of some requirements mobile phone usage in library is inevitable. Library services have changed with the transformations in computing and networking (Cummings, Merrill,Borrelli, 2010), and also under the influence of technology, users' behaviors and expectations in this new environment have changed (Lorcan, 2008). Consequently in order to respond to changes in users' behavior, library environment, communication and telecommunication services, libraries should fundamentally redefine their future functions and services to attract users. The access via mobile phone which is continuously evolving with the users' needs should be regarded as one of the most important factors in formulating the innovative library services in the future (Negishi, 2003). Present library services by the help of mobile technologies and other similar equipments like tablet-pc, makes the bond between library services and users' daily life.

The technologies have made communication and access to information very convenient and time consuming. The users have the comfort of use in their home and office, and from where ever they are while on the move with their mobile phone units or PDAs (Abdul Karim, Darus and Hussain). In recent years the new mobile phones services and facilities have become as important as call making, and even more favorable. In 2009, for the first time ever, mobile phones were used more for accessing data than to making calls (Fox2010).

HISTORY OF MOBILE COMMUNICATION

In the late 1960s till the early 1970s, there was much talk about "generations" of computer hardware — usually "three generations".

First generation : The 1st Generation standard (1G) for voice only was developed in 1979 and the IBM 650 was a first generation computer. Thermionic vacuum tubes. Mid-1940s. IBM pioneered the arrangement of vacuum tubes in pluggable modules.

The second generation (2G) standard using global system for mobile communications

(GSM)/TDMA – time division multiple access, which emerged somewhere in 1992. The generation that follows is based on 2.5G standard known as General Packet Radio Service(GPRS).

3rd Generation or 3G (Abdul Karim, Darus and Hussin , 2006); By 2009, it had become clear that, at some point, 3G networks would be overwhelmed by the growth of bandwidth-intensive applications like streaming media.

4th generation standard was developed. The first two commercially available technologies billed as 4G were the WiMAX standard (en.Wikipedia).

Accordingly, GSMHistory.com has recorded three very distinct 5G network visions that had emerged by 2014:

A super-efficient mobile network that delivers a better performing network for lower investment cost. It addresses the mobile network operators' pressing need to see the unit cost of data transport falling at roughly the same rate as the volume of data demand is rising. It would be a leap forward in efficiency based on the IET Demand Attentive Network (DAN) philosophy.

A super-fast mobile network comprising the next generation of *small cells* densely clustered to give a contiguous coverage over at least urban areas and getting the world to the final frontier of true "wide-area mobility." It would require access to spectrum under 4 GHz perhaps via the world's first global implementation of *Dynamic Spectrum Access*.

A converged fiber-wireless network that uses, for the first time for wireless Internet access, the *millimeter wave* bands (20 – 60 GHz) so as to allow very-wide-bandwidth radio channels able to support data-access speeds of up to 10 Gbit/s. The connection essentially comprises "short" wireless links on the end of local *fiber optic cable*. It would be more a "nomadic" service (like Wi-Fi) rather than a wide-area "mobile" service. (en.Wikipedia).

There was also a parallel set of generations for software:

First generation : Machine language.

Second generation : *Low-level programming languages* such as *Assembly language*. Second generation: Transistors. 1956. The era of miniaturization begins. Transistors are much smaller than vacuum tubes, draw less power, and generate less heat. Discrete transistors are soldered to circuit boards, with interconnections accomplished by stencil-screened conductive patterns on the reverse side. The *IBM 7090* was a second-generation computer.

Third generation: Structured *high-level programming languages* such as *C, COBOL* and *FORTRAN*. Third generation: Integrated circuits (silicon chips containing multiple transistors). 1964. A pioneering example is the ACPX module used in the IBM 360/91, which, by stacking layers of silicon over a ceramic substrate, accommodated over 20 transistors per chip; the chips could be packed together onto a circuit board to achieve unheard-of logic densities. The IBM 360/91 was a hybrid second- and third-generation computer.

Fourth generation: Domain-specific *high-level programming languages* such as *SQL* (for *database* access) and *TeX* (for text formatting)

The term "fifth generation" was intended to convey the system as being a leap beyond existing machines. In the *history of computing hardware*, computers using *vacuum tubes* were called the first generation; *transistors* and *diodes*, the second;

integrated circuits, the third; and those using *microprocessors*, the fourth. Whereas previous computer generations had focused on increasing the number of logic elements in a single CPU, the fifth generation, it was widely believed at the time, would instead turn to massive numbers of CPUs for added performance.

Some of the statistics about mobile users in India

- Telephone subscribers (wireless and landline): 1052.33 million (February 2016)
- Land lines: 25.17 million (February 2016)
- Cell phones: 1027.17 million (February 2016)
- Monthly cell phone addition: 9 million (February 2016)
- Teledensity: 81.82% (November 2015)

In the last few years, India has witnessed a humongous growth in the sales of smart phones due to various design and upto date smart phone coming to market. The Indian debut of many Chinese smart phone manufacturers, likes of Xiaomi, CoolPad, Vivo, Oppo, is resulting in lowering Average Selling Price (ASP). The price sensitive market, as India is known for, is flooded with sub-$150 smart phones has squeezed the upgrade period of feature-to-smart phone. Even, many first-time mobile phone users in India are directly jumping to sub-$90 smartphones. Such trends have helped to the country to witness the fastest ever smart phone growth to 239 million smart phone users by the end of 2015.

The massive adoption of low-price smart phones is allowing the users to carry their digital world with them. The lowing cost of mobile data and free accessibility to the internet via WiFi in many areas, is fascinating smart phone users like never before. Due to wi-fi in Railway station due to Indian Govt.'s decision, people are very much using the smart phone. Consequently, the average consumption of mobile data per smart phone user in India is expected to reach 2.08 GB per month by 2020, up by 384% from mere 430 Mb in 2015, claims Cisco.

The growth in the number of mobile internet users in India and the mobile data consumption in 2016 would largely be influenced by the adoption of smartphone and rich media content. In the country of 1.3 billion people, mobile phone *subscriptions in India* has already reached 1 billion mark, according to the latest data supplied by TRAI. It's the number of mobile internet users and smart phone users in the country that will create big waves in the next few years.

MOBILE TECHNOLOGY

Mobile technologies are characterized by their small size and portability. Mobile technology is exactly what the name indicates – technology that is portable; it refers to any device that you can carry with you to perform a wide variety of "tasks". Mobile devices include smartphones, tablets, and netbooks. It is technology that allows those tasks to be performed via cellular phone, PDA, vehicles, laptops, etc. A standard mobile device has gone from being no more than a simple two-way pager to being a cellular phone, a GPS navigation system, a web browser, and instant messenger system, a video gaming system, and much more. They change the way people communicate since they provide information retrieval and other communication options on a single device. An ever-increasing number of people worldwide access the Internet through their mobile devices daily to read and send e-mails, check the news and weather, do their banking, and access social networks such as Facebook or Twitter. Taking into consideration these mobile devices and their impact on our daily life, the question arises whether those in the Library and Information Science (LIS) community (both librarians and students) are ready to adopt mobile library services. It includes the use of a variety of transmission media such as: radio wave, microwave, infra-red, GPS and Bluetooth to allow for the transfer of data via voice, text, video, 2-dimensional barcodes and more. (C:\Users\LIBRARY\Desktop\Mobile Tech\M.T\What it is\1.htm) Examples of Mobile IT devices include:

- Laptop and netbook computers
- Laptop computers or personal digital assistants
- Mobile Phones and "Smart Phones"
- Global positioning system (GPS) devices
- Wireless debit/credit card payment terminals
- Mobile devices can be enabled to use a variety of communications technologies such as:

- Wireless fidelity (Wi-Fi)- a type of wireless local area network technology
- Bluetooth- Connects mobile devices wirelessly
- Third generation' (3G), global system for mobile communications (GSM) and
- general packet radio service (GPRS) data services- data networking services for mobile phones
- Dial-up services- data networking services using modems and telephone lines.
- Mobile technology extends computing and the Internet into the wireless medium, and provides greater flexibility in communication, collaboration, and information sharing Virtual private networks- secure access to a private network. Conversely, this technology provides unique learning opportunities and has advantage of portability and mobility. Academic, public and special libraries could use mobile technology in service innovations, m-learning, instruction in mobile device, web lectures, reference services and catalogue searching (Sudhir Ramdas Nagarkar)

Association of college research and library (ACRL) report, "2010 top ten trends in academic libraries", has mentioned that explosive growth of mobile devices and applications will drive new services. It was also mentioned in the report that librarian will also need to think creatively about developing services through mobile devices. Many research have been done, which found rapid growth in number of users having mobile devices like Smart phones, e-book readers, iPads, and other handheld devices. Around the world many libraries have started providing services on mobile phones and its positive results are making the way for others to plan for the same. While in Indian scenario it's still in very initial stage. Libraries are trying to connect with SmS alert services to the users. In India still the users of mobile devices suitable for accessing mobile services of library are less in number.

Now a day maximum of library users has the mobile phone with the facility of internet. The library network can authorize them to access the information and other library resources to see or download. The library network can make check and permit to access only authentic user only. Different course like write, read, downloading and payment permeation will be done online. The smart phone works like a PC on internet to getting information from library. Mobile phone has different tools/ programs like Instant Messaging, E-mails, Multimedia tool and other's for access and view/read information's. The Data Placed on library server is in different format like in word, sound, video or a picture and a mobile/smart phone have all tools to view/ read/listen that. So it is a common way to make connection with library users and serving them 24*7.

Due to more use of smartphone, the access via mobile phone which is continuously evolving with the user's needs should be regarded as one of the most important factors in formulating the innovative library services. Present library services by the help of mobile technologies and other similar equipments like tablet-pc, makes the bond between library services and users daily life. Some of the advantages of the mobile library services are Providing library services beyond the location and geographical barriers, The use of smart phone is simpler than PCs and Cost-saving in purchasing soft/hardware. Many information resources have created mobile apps as powerful gateways to their online resources. These apps have different tools for getting information from different information portals. They are used to download or see the information's on mobile phone throw internet facility in anywhere and everywhere as per internet link availability.

Some Mobile apps or Mobile browsers are: -

- iBooks is an iTunes app that includes access to the iBookstore for a wide variety of reading materials.
- The Free Books app provides 23,469 classic titles for selection, and allows for
- Highlighting notes, dictionary support, and bookmarks, which make it an asset for any library.
- The Audiobooks application offers free books that you can listen to for multitasking and hands free enjoyment of books.

- The Kindle is by far the most globally popular e-reader and e-reading app on the market, and was created by Amazon. Due to its connections with Amazon it has a huge selection of books to choose from in a multitude of categories. Create documents for many purposes including library newsletters, documents for handouts and other pages that may need to be printed later with this mobile word processor.
- This free note making app organizes and saves ideas by giving you the opportunity to snap photos, take notes, make voice reminders, and even scan business cards.
- Dropbox is a cloud app that allows you to share files between your mobile phone and
- The computer wherever the app is installed. Although most libraries have Wi-Fi, there isn't always access on the journey between home and work. Offline Pages Pro will give you the opportunity to take information and web pages with you to read or work on while you're not connected to the internet. It also includes PDF reader support.
- Reading is no fun if you don't know meaning of all the words that you are reading, which is why having a dictionary on the go is a great tool for a librarian. This app also works as a thesaurus and offers a word of the day for each day of the week to strengthen your vocabulary and keep things interesting.
- Wikipedia may not always be 100% guaranteed correct information, but it's an excellent resource for librarians in a pinch who need to look up an answer to a question of a patron. It is one of the largest online information sources across the globe, so it has a little bit of everything, and Wikipanion was designed to easily access the information in Wikipedia. It is great for research related to academic projects going on within the library, and it is also helpful as a library patron aid for those who come to do school work.
- The Mango Mobile Library Edition helps with language learning and is free for both iPhone and Android users.

With this app you can take cultural lessons and hear the proper pronunciation of words by native speakers. This is an Android application that can be great for librarians who want to look up a certain person, place, or item, but can't think of the name. You simply take a photo using your mobile device and then Google Goggles will search for it in its database and give you some information about it if it is found in its database.

LITERATURE REVIEW

Neghishi (2003) in "development of Mobile Phone Culture in Japan and Its Implications to Library Services: Prospecting Information Services in Coming "Ubiquitous Society" reviewed mobile phone infrastructure development in Japan and consequently it's application in Japanese university libraries including I-book service in library of Toyoma university. Iwhiwhu, Ruteyan& Eghwubare(2010) discussed mobile phone application in library services with an emphasis on Delta Stat university library and enumerates some of applications and views about it. The result of Abdulkarim, Daroos & Hussein(2006)'s article about "Mobile phone applications in academic library services" showed many respondent's willingness to receive benefits of mobile phones services.

Marato and Fang (2010) in the article of "Mobile Phone Access in Sub-Saharan Africa: Research and A Library Proposal" showed application of these services among villagers and farmers. Camings, Meril & Borrelli, (2010) in the article about the use of handheld mobile devices, their impact and implications for library services showed that 58.4 percent of respondents who owned a web-enabled handheld device indicated that they would use small screen devices, such as PDAs or web-enabled cell phones to search a library OPAC. M.lever, E. Katz(2006) surveyed American great university libraries policy responses to an invasive mobile technology, the results showed that libraries adopt an array of stances when approaching cell phone use within their library facilities. These approaches included structured guidelines that specifically address cell phone use posted on the library website, signs displayed throughout the library barring cell phone use, and signage that provides patrons with a list of areas in which use is permitted.

Moyo(2004) indicates that digital reference service will also offer the following benefits:

- service will be accessible wherever there is Internet access;
- capability to reach both remote and local library users;
- increased accessibility of librarians to library users;
- point-of-need assistance to users;
- convenience for those users who cannot otherwise come to the library (e.g. mobility impaired, invalids, etc.);
- expanded scope of library services while extending hours of service (facilitates 24/7 service);
- additional communication option for library users;
- opportunity to market the library to virtual communities and, meeting of user expectations (library users expect the library to offer competitive online services like banking, shopping, investment and so on).

SOME OF THE MOBILE SERVICE

Wireless easy communication: One of the most important and basic features of a mobile phone is that it provides wireless connection among people for communication in the information age. People can contact each other from anywhere/anytime as per need. Moreover, with the help of data cable, it can be used as a modem to access Internet by connecting it to your PC or laptop. If you have activated Internet service in your mobile phone you can surf Internet in your mobile phone.

Wi-Fi : Connect to Internet wirelessly anywhere within a mobile phone network and reap the benefits and ease of accessing Internet within a limited geographical space. Technology has made the mobile phones more usable than laptops and desktops. Now it's not necessary to carry a laptop or be seated on a desktop to connect to internet and download your required piece of information which only can be downloaded within library premises. It will reduce the problem of limited resources (space and hardware) against the limitless users of a library. And user will also feel free to come anytime to the library for information access, as it's possible that one can forget his laptop, pen drive and other storing devices but very rarely the mobile phone. Smart phones with Wi-Fi technology are very useful to provide library services within the libraries with limited resources and can use as per need.

Internet access : With the help of new mobile phone technology one can easily access internet form anywhere and everywhere. No need to stay at home and connect-disconnect to the network every time before and after using the network. Constant network connection is the best feature of a mobile for a 21st generation's user. GPS (Global Positioning System) which helps in finding location can be used in libraries for locating materials inside the libraries. There are so many electronic gadget available for automation of libraries for Smartphone's users.

SMS & MMS : Short Message service or text messaging is a method of exchanging brief messages with others. Not only text messages but picture and video messages which are also known as Multimedia message service (MMS) technology. SMS alert can be used for users to inform them about various many others. Users can be informed about the exhibitions organized by the libraries and their queries about libraries and their information and library could disseminate the information through these medium as per user's demand.

Memory cards : Simple mobile phones have a memory which is used for saving contacts and text messages. However, from 2G to smart phones, this device is accompanied with memory cards. Previously memory cards were of 2GB-4GB but now the capacity increased up to 32GB. You can store all forms of information like audio, video and text. Mostly memory cards are used for storing mp3 files and videos; however, these can be used to store any kind of information of your use (articles, e-books, educational mp3 and videos) so that you can access it anywhere you want. The card can be removed and used in computer with the help of memory card readers. The memory card can be used as a storing device for information downloaded within the library, no need to bring pen drives as it's not safe to use pen drives in public. And no need to bring CD or disks for storing information, only your mobile phone is more than enough.

Cloud storage : Technical advancements have aided the smart phones with free online storage (also called cloud storage) through services such as Dropbox. It has made your available information storage space limitless; assured your important data safety and recovery, in case your phone is broken or stolen. And because your files are stored online it's easy to share it with others and accessible from anywhere and anytime.

Bluetooth : Now a day's Bluetooth is a common feature of mobile phones through which user can easily transfer data wirelessly within a short area network connection. It works on short range radio transmission technology, through which two devices can connect and transfer data to each other. It can be used for data transfer in libraries.

Wireless Application Protocol (WAP) : Wireless refers to radio transmission of data, the software designed to fulfill this specific purpose can be said as the application, and protocol is the standard or set of rules to be followed while data transmission. Over all we can say that WAP is a standard for providing wireless internet access and advanced telephony services to the mobile device users.

NFC : It is same like Bluetooth, used for wireless data transfer over very short distance. It is much faster than Bluetooth. It is upgraded RFID system which connects the interface of a smartcard and reader in to a single device and allows the user to transfer data without any interruption. Due to its shorter range it is safer than Bluetooth.

IM : Instant messaging is a service which provides the users with immediate communication or conversation through mobile phone to a person online in the place of emails. Email sending includes certain steps to be followed every time and its time taking for sending short messages and having real time conversation with a person. So the instant messaging has become popular among the mobile users. IM and SMS both can be used for the reference service from a library like "ASK A LIBRARIAN". Researcher can submit their reference request through SMS or IM and reference librarian can also provide the service in same way. Book recommendations according to the user's interest can be sent through IM and SMS. For this service users profile along with their mobile numbers can be prepared. All these above mentioned features have changed the mobile phone form a simple communicating device to handheld computing device. These new features have increased its usability in various library services.

SOCIAL NETWORKING SITES (FACEBOOK, MYSPACE, TWITTER)

Facebook, MySpace and Twitter are three prominent social networking sites. Lenhart and Madden (2007) found that 67% of young adults aged 18–32 used social networking sites; Rideout et. al. (2010) found that 53% of 15–18 year olds used social networking websites. An average of 48 minutes is spent per day on the sites (Oladokun, 2015). According to Onyango (2012), the dramatic penetration of the social networking activity in Africa was made possible by the fact that 57% of tweets are emanating from mobile devices. There is a significant change to the figures in the study of Farooqi, et. al. (2013) which found that of the 1000 participants whose age ranged from 18–25 years, 640 or 64% of them were using Facebook daily for around 3–4 hours. It is palpable that within these age brackets are university students doing their diploma, degree or higher degree programmes either full-time, part-time or by ODL mode.

Skype/ooVoo

According to Barnhart and Pierce (2011), video communication tools, such as Skype and OoVoo, are being used for professional communications in both higher education and industry, and have already been piloted as reference tools by some libraries. According to Olivas and Chan (2013), the California State University San Marcos education librarian began using Skype as a way to meet 'face-to-face" with distance education masters and doctoral students who could not come to campus because of how far they lived or because of time constraints. They indicate that like Google talk and other voice-over Internet protocol tools, Skype offers voice and video capabilities enabling the users to have a conversation with each other during real time.

Library Anywhere

Created and sold through LibraryThing, Library Anywhere is a mobile catalog for any library. Includes mobile Web and apps for iPhone, Blackberry, and Android. Prices range from $150 annually for schools to $1,000 annually for universities (additional fees may apply). Access: http://www.librarything.com/forlibraries.

MobileTuts+

Tutorials for all mobile developers, regardless of platform. Topics include techniques for building mobile apps and mobile Web sites.Access: http://mobile.tutsplus.com/.

MobiSiteGalore

Build a mobile Web site in less than 60 minutes. No technical or programming knowledge required. Packages range from basic (cost: free) to unlimited (cost: $24.99 per month). Access:http://www.mobisitegalore.com.

MoFuse

Build a mobile version of an existing Web site or blog with the MoFuse (short for Mobile Fusion) content management platform. Plans range from $7.95 per month to $199 per month. All accounts come with a 14-day risk-free trial. Access: http://mofuse.com/.

Blogs

Blogs have several potential uses by academic libraries. Blogs can be used to communicate library events, publicize information resources, and offer subject-related reference services (Zhipping and Yan, 2009). Microblogging, which is a newer blog option made popular by Twitter, allows librarians to go where the students are located. Unlike traditional blogs, Librarians can interact and respond to student comments without the requirement that students visit the official library web site (Dickson and Holley, 2010). However, for blogs to be an effective method of interaction, librarians need to respond quickly to any comments posted on the library account.

MOBILE WEB SITES

In addition to or in place of mobile applications, some companies and organizations also develop mobile versions of their Web site that are better optimized for viewing on mobile devices.

Encyclopedia Britannica Mobile. Offers a search box and a list of suggested searches. Results include full-text entries with enlargeable images. Access: http://i.eb.com/.

MedlinePlus Mobile. Produced by the U.S. National Library of Medicine, MedlinePlus Mobile provides information about specific diseases, conditions, and wellness issues. The site also contains prescription drug information, medical dictionary, and current health news. Access: http://m.medlineplus.gov.

WorldCat Mobile. Search the WorldCat catalog for books, movies, music, games, and more. Results include items available at local libraries. Access: http://www.worldcat.org (Sudesh Kumar Sood & Ipshita Mukherjee, 2013)

ADVANTAGES OF MOBILE SERVICES

Some of the advantages of the mobile library services in the 21st generation age are:

- Providing library services beyond the location and geographical barriers.
- The use of Cell phones is simpler than PCs and will be more smarter than Personal Computer of 20th Century.
- Cost-saving in purchasing soft/hardware (compared with computers particularly laptops).
- High influence coefficient.
- Easy to handle and movable with the users and will use multiple work like calling to stcring.

The benefits of using mobile devices and smart phones in library services can be explained with the help of five laws of the library science defined by Dr. S. R Ranganathan:

- **Books are for use :** Making the library content and OPAC mobile accessible through mobile devices, in the format these devices support, is qualifying the first law of library science. As the new generation users want the content in electronic format and accessible through their choice of device. If the library has a huge coilection, it should also be in the form which more of it user would like to access. Only having huge collection will not make the use possible but the format is also a remarkable factor in present technological era. Due the fact that many electronic devices for reading e-books are available for example Kindle, Nook, Sony e-book reader.

- **Every reader his/her book :** Availability of books, information, and needful library services on the user's choice of device (mobile device) and format (mobile supported) so that they can access it from anywhere/ anytime they want.
- **Every book its user :** catalogue of a library represents the collection it has on different subjects. As the serving medium is changing from traditional to mobile, Mobile OPACs are best to serve this purpose. Many libraries are trying to make smart phone applications for the library OPAC. Informing the users of new arrivals through IM and SMS services will also serve purpose.
- **Save the time of user :** As the user of information and library content is depending on mobile devices for retrieving information. The content should also be made mobile device compatible to reach the user at their place from anywhere and anytime. Users need not to move towards the library every time for accessing information, it saves the time of users. The databases, reference guides, and other sources of information of a library can be made accessible through mobile devices. Facility of booking documents through SMS, Many libraries have already started working on this concept.
- **Library is a growing organism :** Growing in all contexts whether it is collection, space, infrastructure due to new technological innovations, and services only to satisfy the user's need. From traditional/manual to machinery, machinery to computer, and now from desktop to mobile devices, the library and library services are growing with the new developments and need of the user. It is not only

providing growth but relevance also to the library in present era.

Besides qualifying the five laws of library science it has some other benefits as follows:

Low cost implication : It requires less amount than operating computer based services in library. As they have to provide only the services to the users the retrieval device is with users. And unlike the computer the possibility of having mobile devices and smart phones in present context is more.

Connect with user directly : Services on mobile devices provide the facility of connecting librarian with users directly through IM and SMS services and developing new applications for accessing different library services on smart phones.

ICT SKILLS REQUIRED

Librarians should acquire and apply the following skills for providing mobile-based services:

- Knowledge of hardware and software of mobile devices
- Create/tailor mobile-optimized content including interactive and participative library homepages, OPAC, virtual tours, and databases
- Familiarity with internet/intranet services like using e-mail, SMS and spam preventing, etc.
- Develop expertise in protecting privacy and security levels as more personalised information is involved in using mobiles for library services
- Skills related to searching and navigating through mobile devices, mobile web applications like push e-mail, etc.
- Skills for interacting with users via smart phone applications, mobile-friendly webpages, and third party intermediary clients
- Skills relating to training and user orientation to market these services to users. (Malathy S. and Kantha P, 2013)

INNOVATION STRATEGY FOR MOBILE SERVICES

The ten target areas identified in the Library mobile strategy included a number in each innovation arena:

- development of a mobile search interface
- adoption of QR codes
- investigation of an instant messaging enquiry service
- investigation of SMS/text messaging Library notices and Enquiry Service
- mobile e-book strategy
- evaluation of Bluetooth technology
- mobile infrastructure within Library buildings
- development of a mobile user education strategy
- development of a mobile promotion and evaluation strategy
- development of Live Lab concept for device and service testing.

PROBLEMS AND NEED OF LIBRARY SERVICES THROUGH MOBILE TECHNOLOGY

Leaves out non-mobile device users : Services through mobile device has chances that it will leave out the non mobile device users. The users having mobile devices will only be benefited through these services. Users itself need to have devices for using these services.

Network problems in smart phone services : Fluctuation of mobile network is another obstacle in providing services through smart phones and mobile phones like IM and SMS services.

Need of skilled staff : Providing services through mobile need skilled staff having the knowledge of making the content of library available through mobile devices.

Need of user awareness : Now a days users are less interested in visiting library to access information.

- Problem like Slow Connectivity always faced by mobile users.
- There are different platform for run library apps on mobile.
- Different Font Standards of different mobiles.
- Data Cost is increasing.

- Excess use of mobile devises may be harmful to eyes and overall health.

However, the libraries itself are trying to reach the users on their mobile devices because the time's demand. But there is a need of user awareness for these kinds of services. Libraries have to do marketing of their services to popularize them among the library users from academic community to public community to optimal utilization of library resources and training program for users is also needed to make the user aware of services, where the new users will not take any negativity using the smartphones.

CONCLUSION

The rapid increase in mobile phone usage has revolutionized the information communication in many fold. Due to smart phones are selling as low cost and application technology is fastly updated, therefore every alternate day, new technology smart phones are coming to market by various companies.

Mobile phones are inevitable tools of Information Communication Technology. Application of mobile phones to provide library and information services will open new pathway towards this trend in the coming age. To cope up with the demand of new advancements in communication technology libraries are also trying to reconstruct their services as per global demand. Mobile devices have added new dimensions to the library services in this way. In this age of running life when people have no time to visit library frequently, mobile devices are working as time saver for them by making ease of accessing library collection from anywhere and anytime. A library may reach the remote users effectively by adopting mobile technology in its services. Library policies and services should be flexible and open so that new information needs of users are met with new technologies. The task of libraries is to exploit new technology in a more effective way to promote and integrate them into the design of future library services in a cost efficient manner. Apart from this, services through mobile devices can help in keeping the relevance of library in present era. Another important issue is providing library services through mobile devices sounds good but not so easy. It will need specialized staff, different setup, and user awareness etc. when library moves on wheel along with its content to reach user, it's called Mobile Library, but now the library collection and the services are made mobile to reach the user at their place through mobile devices. It has merits and demerits both, but the big thing is the need of technological era's library users.

REFERENCES

1. ACRL (2008). Guidelines for Distance Learning Library Services. Available at: http://www.ala.org/acrl/standards/guidelines distancelearning Retrieved June 15, 2015
2. Aoki, K., & Pogroszewski, D. (1998). Virtual university reference model: A guide to delivering education and support services to the distance learner. Online journal of distance learning administration, 1(3). Retrieved from http://www.westga.edu/~distance/ojdla/fall13/aoki13.html
3. Azubuike, A. A. (2006). The world summit on the information society: Issues and the way forward for Nigerian libraries. Paper presented at the Nigerian Library Association 44th Annual conference and AGM, Abuja, Nigeria. Retrieved from http://www.nlang. org/abuja2006compedium.pdf#page=50
4. Barnhart, F., & Pierce, J. (2011). Becoming Mobile: Reference in the Ubiquitous Library. Journal of Library Administration. 51(3), 279-290,
5. Chu, M., & Meulemans, Y. N. (2008). The problems and potential of MySpace and Facebook usage in academic libraries. Internet Reference Services Quarterly, 13(1), 69-85.
6. Chu, S. K.-W., & Du, H. S. (2013). Social networking tools for academic libraries. Journal of Librarianship and Information Science, 45(1), 64-75.
7. Constine, J. (2014). Facebook Hits 100M Users in Africa, half the continent's Internetconnected population. Available online at: http://techcrunch.com/2014/09/08/facebookafrica/Retrieved 10 June 2015
8. Dhara Sharma and Mr. Dipti Ranjan Sahoo (2014).International Journal of Information Technology and Library Science.ISSN 2349-235X Volume 3, Number 1, pp. 17-24 http://www.ripublication.com
9. Ezeani, C. N., & Igwesi, U. (2012). Using social media for dynamic

library service delivery: The Nigeria experience. Library Philosophy and Practice. Paper 814. Retrieved from http://digitalcommons.unl.edu/cgi/viewcontent.cgi?article=2011&context=libphilprac

10. Farooqi, H. et al. (2013). Effect of Facebook on the life of medical university students.

11. International Archives of Medicine Vol. 6(1):40. doi: 10.1186/1755-7682-6-40. Available at: http://www.ncbi.nlm.nih.gov/pubmed/24134850

12. Fox, Megan K "PDAs, Handhelds and Mobile Technologies in Libraries", available at http://web.simmons.edu/~fox/pda/

13. Fox, Megan K. "Trends in Mobile Tools & Applications for Libraries", available at http://web.simmons.edu/~fox/pda/semrls_07.pdf

14. Giles, Nicola, and Sue Grey-Smith. 2005. Txting librarians @ curtin., available at http://conferences. alia.org.au/online2005/papers/al2.pdf.

15. Golvin, Charles S. (2007). "The iPhone Is A Win-Win-Win", Forrester Research

16. Herman, S. (2007). SMS reference: keeping up with your clients The Electronic Library, 25(4),401-408.

17. Golvin, C. S. (2008). Which generations are doing mobile data activities, 2007. Forrester Research,January 4, 2008.

18. Greifender, E., & Cuong Linh, N. (2008). A survey of the application of Web 2.0 in

19. Australasian university libraries. Library Hi Tech, 26(4), 630-653.

20. Herman, S. (2007). SMS reference: keeping up with your clients The Electronic Library, 25(4), 401-408.

21. Houghton, Sarah. (2005a). Heavyweights beware: Alternatives to traditional virtual reference products, available at http://www.co.marin.ca.us/library/HeavyweightsBeware.ppt.

22. Houghton, Sarah. (2005b). Text a librarian: Integrating reference by SMS into digital reference: Virtual reference desk conference, available at http://librarianinblack.typepad.com/librarianinblack/2005/1l/text_a_libraria.htm.

23. Libraries offering SMS reference services. (2007). Online Reference. Library Success:A Best Practices Wiki, available at http://www.libsuccess.org/indexphp?title=Online_Reference#Librades_Offering_SMS_Reference_Services.

24. Jack, M. M. (2006). Library 2.0 Theory: Web 2.0 and Its Implications for Libraries. Webology, 3 (2), 25.

25. JISC Strategy infoKit: http://www.jiscinfonet.ac.uk/Infokits/strategy(accessed 30 June 2011).

26. Karim, N. S. A., Darus, S. H. and Hussin, R. (2006). Mobile phone applications in academic library services: a students' feedback survey. Campus-Wide Information Systems, 23(1),35-51.

27. Kroski, E. (2008a). Library mobile initiatives. Library Technology Reports,44(5), 33-38.

28. Kroski, E. (2008b).What can you do with the mobile web. Library Technology Reports, 44(5),16-32.

29. Kroski, E. (2008c). What is the mobile web? Library Technology Reports, 44(5), 5-9.

30. Kroski, E. (n.d.). On the move with mobile web: Libraries and mobile technologies, available at http://www.ellyssakroski.com.

31. Lippincott, J K A(2010). Mobile Future for Academic Libraries, References Services Review, 38 Library Success (n.d.). M-Libraries, available at http://www.libsuccess.org/index.php?title=M- 2), 205–213.

32. Malathy S and Kantha P(2013). Application of Mobile Technologies to Libraries. DESIDOC Journal of Library & Information Technology. (Sept);33(5): 361-366

33. Mayank Trivedi and Vishnu Suthar(2011). A plan of M-Library for Smt. Hansa Mehta Library: A study. International Journal of Information and Communication Technology Research. (July); 1(3): 91-95 ISSN-2223-4985

34. Mohan Lal Vishwakarma, Shyam Lal Maurya & Shivani Govil (2013). Use of Mobile Technology in Indian Libraries. International Journal of Engineering and Computer Science ISSN: 2319-7242. (June); 2(6): 1799-1805

35. Sudhir Ramdas Nagarkar(2011). Use of Mobile Technology in Library services. Indian Streams Research Journal. (Dec); 3(11): 1-4 ISSN No : 2230-7850

36. Sudesh Kumar Sood and Ipsita Mukherjee (2013). Mobile technology in emerging library and information services. Conference Papers; 1st SPL Annual Convention (NCLTDP-2013), Agra, Y K Publishers, , p I 211-I 218, ISBN978-93-80668-21-5

37. Tucker, R B (2008). Driving growth through innovation (2nd ed), San Francisco, Berrett-Koehler.

38. Whelan, David P(2006). A technology sampler platter. Library Hi Tech News 23 (2006): 25-26.

2

Digital Preservation Methods and its Merits and Demerits

Muthumathi Dharuman*

ABSTRACT

Digital Preservation is one of the urgent challenges in libraries in this digital era. Preservation is the current trends in all modern libraries and a recognized as a vital part of managing information in digital format. Preservation in library and information science is concerned with maintaining or restoring access to books, documents and records through the study, diagnosis, treatment and prevention of decay and damage. The concept of preservation knows how to be characterized as communication with the future. It is known that in the future new technology will be used that is more cost effective and more sophisticated than modern technology. Digital preservation is about a series of actions that need to be taken and managed to make sure there is continued access to digital materials for as long as is necessary. As long as is necessary could mean long term - into the indefinite future, or short-term – for a specific time limited business requirement.

This strategy delivers a framework within which technical solutions for library content can be developed and

* Chief Librarian, Velammal Medical College Hospital & Research Institute, Madurai, Tamilnadu

implemented to mitigate the technical risks associated with longevity, whilst simultaneously addressing the cultural and organisational challenges required to ensure continuous and consistent management of the digital collections throughout their entire lifecycle.

Keywords: Digital library, Digital Objects, Digital Preservation

INTRODUCTION

ALA(2009) Defines, 'Digital preservation combines policies, strategies and actions that ensure access to digital content overtime'.

We are living in a digital world. Computers now far outnumber office workers in many parts of the globe. Most information is now "born digital", Much is disseminated only in digital form. The digital world transforms traditional preservation concepts from protecting the physical integrity of the object to specifying the creation and maintenance of the object whose intellectual integrity is its primary characteristic. This transformation, along with the new leadership possibilities it creates, will force librarians and archivists to transform their services and programs in turn. Primary objective of digital preservation in Library is maintaining the ability to meaningfully access digital collection content over time. As well as collecting digital materials and managing them for current access, the Library has a mandate and commitment to preservation and has been active in developing infrastructure to collect, manage, preserve and keep digital collections available into the future

In the last two decades, digital technology has enabled us to create, use, and be enriched by information in ways that were unthinkable a generation ago. Digital technology and high speed networks are leading to sweeping changes throughout the society. In the past few years significant progress has been made to define the terms and outline a research agenda for preserving digital information that was either originally or transformed to digital form. Traditional sources of information are increasing every day and the users expectations are to save the valuable information at safer place. Digital technologies present a preservation solution for the documents in the libraries with increased access to digitized documents over the electronic networks. Digital technology as well as all others associated with Internet and web technologies is a continuous flux of change.

DIGITISATION

Digitization of library collection has become a common activity among academic libraries. Libraries, more particularly academic libraries are realizing the need to make available their local collection in digital forms to their users apart from subscribing to digitized resources in terms of online databases and e-books,. Academic libraries have always been the depositories of intellectual contents such as theses, dissertations, research reports, students' projects and various published and unpublished works of the faculty members, staff and students. In this context digitization has become bare necessities for academic libraries in digital environment.

According to Arms, a digital library is a managed collection of information with associated services where the information is stored in digital format and accessible over a network.

A digital library is an organized collection of digitized material or it's holding in the digital form, which can be accessible by a computer on the network. It is a later stage of electronic library. In digital library high speed optical fiber are used for LAN and the access is over WAN and provide a wide range of Internet based services i.e. audio and video conferencing and like other. The majority of the holding of a digital library is in the computer

Witten and David (2003) defined Digitization as the process of taking traditional library materials that are in form of books and papers and converting them to the electronic form where they can be stored and manipulated by a computer.

Ding, Choo Ming (2000) has elaborated the works of Getz (1997), Line (1996) and Mckinley (1997) on the Merits of digitization. They maintained that:

- Digitization means no new buildings are required; information sharing can be enhanced and redundancy of collections reduced.

- Digitization leads to the development of Internet in digitalized based libraries. As Internet is now the preferred form of publication and dissemination.
- Digital materials can be sorted, transmitted and retrieved easily and quickly.
- Access to electronic information is cheaper than its print counterpart when all the files are stored in an electronic warehouse with compatible facilities and equipment.
- Digital texts can be linked, thus made interactive; besides, it enhances the retrieval of more information.

REASONS FOR DIGITISATION

One reason for using digital library technology is to manage huge amounts of digital content such as thousands of images or hundreds of audio clips. Advances in storage technologies have enabled huge amounts of content to be made accessible locally at increasingly reasonable costs. While discussions previously storage of data is on megabytes, now it is not unusual to consider gigabytes and even terabytes. In contrast, 635MB is needed for a typical one hour, stereo quality audio compact disc and 720MB for a standard one hour videotape. Documents and other materials housed in collections are deteriorating at a rapid rate.

Another reason to use digital libraries is the need to be able to perform searches that are impossible manually. The huge amounts of information being created and stored each day makes it that much more difficult to find specific information later. Adding to this are images and multimedia content which present even more challenges for retrieval. There are electronic tools which enable this to be done quickly and easily by text search and also by actually searching on the colors, shapes in images and textures Library materials especially images, old manuscripts, theses, and musical recordings etc. that are in danger of being lost in the future and which are mostly historical and valuable needs to be preserved for future use.

Gertz (2000) outlined that when considering materials for digitization, first criteria will be physical condition of the materials, followed by access, value of content, the demand for the materials, the intellectual property rights, the required infrastructure, cost and sources of funding.

- To facilitate new forms of access and use.
- Better and enhanced access to a defined stock of research material
- Creation of a single point of access to documentation from different institutions concerning a special subject
- Support for democratic considerations by making public records more widely accessible
- Better search and retrieval facilities for library types of materials.
- To give the institution opportunities for the development of its technical infrastructure and staff skill capacity.

FACTORS OF CHANGE TO DIGITAL LIBRARIES

- The limited buying power of libraries
- complex nature of recent document
- storage problem
- Information explosion
- Searching problem in traditional libraries
- Low cost of technology - cost of technologies is much more less than that of traditional libraries.
- Environmental factor - The cleanest technologies to fulfill the slogan 'Burn a CD-ROM save a tree'

DIGITAL PRESERVATION METHODS, MERITS & DEMERITS

Many methods for preserving digital materials have been proposed to combat the approaching disintegration of information. The following Methods are available for digital preservation.

(a) Bit stream copying

Commonly its known as "backing up data" refers to the process of making an exact duplicate of a digital object. In its simplest form, a digital object consists of a bitstream, i.e. an ordered sequence of bits (binary zeros and ones). This binary inscription will usually be stored on a physical medium of some kind. A computer system with the correct combination of hardware or software translates the bitstream into something meaningful. Though a necessary component of all digital preservation strategies, bit-stream copying in itself is not a long-term maintenance technique, since it deals only with the question of data loss due to hardware and media failure, whether resulting from normal malfunction and decay, malicious destruction or natural disaster.

Merits

- Fast data transfers
- Can ignore minor data read errors on source drive
- More complex preservation actions can be carried out
- Preserving the bitstream may be all that is feasible

De-merits

- Requires as much storage as original disk or data
- Tools might not collect marginal (bad) sectors

(b) Migration

Migration is the preservation approach which has been most widely practiced to date. It is defined as the copying or conversion of digital objects from one technology to another, whilst preserving their significant properties. Migration focuses on the digital object itself, rather than its environment; it aims to change the object in such a way that hardware and software devel-opments will not affect its accessibility. In Simple term The periodic transfer of digital materials from one hardware/ software configuration to another or from one generation of computer technology to a subsequent generation. It Transfer preserved resources to new generation technology. The purpose of migration is to preserve the integrity of digital objects and to retain the ability of users to retrieve, display, and use them in the face of constantly changing technology.

Merits

- The risks of "availability of operating systems" and "availability of software" are dealt with.

- The risk of format ageing is dealt with.
- The information is preserved in a new, contemporary format
- It is a widely used strategy and procedures for simple migration are well established.
- It is generally a reliable way to preserve the intellectual content of digital objects and is particularly suited to page-based documents.
- Conversion software for some formats is readily available.

Demerits

- Very expensive due to assessment of formats and observation of the development of formats
- Continuous task which needs to be repeated on a regular basis
- It does not protect against obsolescence of devices and data carriers. Information may be lost during migration.
- It requires a large commitment of resources, both initially and over time.
- There may be potential IPR problems if either the source or the new format is proprietary
- Specialised conversion tools are needed to convert digital objects from one format to an-other

(c) Refreshing

Refreshing means transferring or copying digital information from one long-term storage medium to another of the same type, with no change whatsoever in the bit-stream that is of concern to the application and operating system using the data (e.g. from a decaying 4mm DAT tape to a new 4mm DAT tape, or from an older CD-RW to a new CD-RW).

Merits

- The risk of "data carrier failure" is dealt with.
- The risk of "availability of reproducers" is dealt with.
- Inexpensive to implement
- Easy to implement

- May reduce the need for refreshing digital contents
- help diminish losses from media deterioration

Demerits

- Problem of dependence on software not solved
- Problem of format ageing not solved
- Not sustainable without combination with other dp strategies
- Durable media has the potential for endangering content by providing a false sense of security.
- Copying from medium to medium, however, also suffers limitations as a means of digital preservation.

(d) Emulation

According to van der Hoeven, "Emulation does not focus on the digital object, but on the hard- and software environment in which the object is rendered. It aims at (re)creating the environment in which the digital object was originally created"[1]

The process of setting up a system to perform in the same way as another system of a different type in order to run its programs. It involves preserving the original application program. Emulation uses a special type of software, called an emulator, to translate instructions from original software to execute on new platforms. Simply said, Imitate old hardware and software environment by means of an emulator" Emulation allows the original application software to be used without requiring the original system to be maintained.

Merits

- The risks of "availability of operating systems" and "availability of software" are dealt with.
- The risk of format ageing is dealt with.
- Data can to a great extent be used as originally.
- The emulation approach can be implemented at a higher level, emulation could be useful as a backup mechanism

Demerits

- Very costly and expensive
- A large number of different emulators are required
- It is not certain that emulators will run on future operating and file systems.
- Emulation has not been widely tested as a long-term digital preservation strategy
- May require the user to master completely unfamiliar technology in order to understand an archival digital record, and technological developments
- Most emulation approaches will involve preserving or emulating proprietary software which is covered by patent, licence or other IPR. This is a major issue.
- Validation needed in any action that transforms file formats to ensure content and reliability that the intellectual content is the same.
- Might be difficult to assure quality of original files without a substantial amount of work to compare the original file to the file after emulation

(e) Encapsulation

It is a technique of grouping together a digital object and anything else necessary to provide access to that object. Encapsulation aims to overcome the problems of the technological obsolescence of file formats by making the details of how to interpret the digital object part of the encapsulated information.

This method maintains that preserved objects should be self-describing, virtually "linking content with all of the information required for it to be deciphered and understood"[2] The files associated with the digital object would have details of how to interpret that object by using "logical structures called "containers" or "wrappers" to provide a relationship between all information components[3] that could be used in future development of emulators, viewers or converters through machine readable specifications. The method of encapsulation is usually applied to collections that will go unused for long periods of time[4]

Merits

- It ensures content and contextual information is stored together, minimising the risk of losing valuable information.
- Metadata stored in the object itself (instead of an external location), that can be easily transferred and migrated with the object means information integrity, provenance, and authenticity are more likely to be preserved.
- It also means the digital objects are "self-descriptive and autonomous: they identify and document themselves"[5].
- It can also aid emulation (as the software needed to be emulated becomes more complex over time), and makes migration of digital objects easier.

Demerits

- Encapsulation is that it relies heavily on standards to maintain readability
- No computer technical standards have yet shown any likelihood of lasting forever indeed most have become completely obsolete within a couple of software generations"
- It is also not great for binary file formats because "there is usually too little space and an expansion of the fields could cause interchangeability and readability problems.
- Metadata to binary files also requires a separate module or software tool for each format, because usually such a functionality is not supported by current computer programs"

(f) Technology Preservation

Preserving hardware and software used to create and access information (i.e. reel-to-reel film and eight-track tape machines). It is based on preserving the technical environment that runs the system, including operating systems, original application software, media drives, etc. It is sometimes called the "computer museum" solution. It involves preserving the digital object together with all the actual hardware and software required to maintain access to the object; this includes operating systems, original application software and media drives. It offers the potential of coping with media obsolescence, assuming the media has not decayed beyond readability. It can extend the access for obsolete media and file formats, but is ultimately a dead end, since no obsolete technology can be kept functional indefinitely.

Merits

- This may be the best solution at least in the short-term because it ensures that the material is accessible by preserving the access tools as well as the object itself

Demerits

- Cost and space implications for acquiring and maintaining large quantities of hard-ware are prohibitive for many organi-sations.
- Older operating system and application software and appropriate licenses must also be acquired and maintained.
- Over time the machines will degrade and ultimately fail, so the number of machines capable of reading certain types of old files will continually decrease.
- Technical support for both software and hardware will also disappear over time.
- Documentation for older computing environments can be difficult to locate.

(g) Digital Archaeology

Digital archaeology involves retrieving data from obsolete software or hardware environments, and obsolete or damaged media, such as punch cards, 8" floppy disks and the wealth of other remova-ble media which have been used since the earliest days of computing. Digital archaeology is explicitly an emergency recovery strategy and usually involves specialized techniques to recover bit-streams from media that has been rendered unreadable, either due to physical damage or hardware failure such as head crashes or magnetic tape crinkling. It is generally carried out by for profit data recovery companies that maintain a variety of storage hardware (including obsolete types) plus special facilities such as clean rooms for dismantling hard disk drives. Given enough resources, readable bit-streams can often be recovered even from heavily damaged media (especially magnetic media), but if the content is old enough, it may not be possible to make it renderable and /or understandable.

Merits

- The value of removable media as art effects, especially if the record creator has annotated media labels.
- They constitute the 'original' version of the digital object.
- The future researcher may wish to experience the original environment.
- Future developments in technology may mean that more data can be extracted from the media.

Demerits

- Disks and other removable media are equivalent to the original files or packaging in which traditional archives arrive at the repository.
- The media will fail with time, as will the devices needed to read them, and maintain-ing the necessary hardware to read old media involves all the demerits associ-ated with technology preservation.
- Much more costly than the other major preservation strategies
- Relying on digital archaeology means that the digital material which isn't necessarily highly valued might not be rescued.

(h) Analogue backups

Analogue backups combine the conversion of digital objects into analogue form with the use of durable analogue media, e.g., taking high-quality printouts or the creation of silver halide microfilm from digital images. An analogue copy of a digital object can, in some respects, preserve its content and protect it from obsolescence, without sacrificing any digital qualities, including shareability and lossless transferability. Text and monochromatic still images are the most amenable to this kind of transfer. Given the cost and limitations of analogue backups, and their relevance to only certain classes of documents, the technique only makes sense for documents whose contents merit the highest level of redundancy and protection from loss.

(i) Canonicalisation

Canonicalization is a technique designed to allow determination of whether the essential characteristics of a document have remained intact through a conversion from one format to another. Canonicalization relies on the creation of a representation of a type of digital object that conveys all its key aspects in a highly deterministic manner. Once created, this form could be used to algorithmically verify that a converted file has not lost any of its essence. Canonicalization has been postulated as an aid to integrity testing of file migration, but it has not been implemented.

(j) Open archiving Information System(OAIS)

An archive, consisting of an organization of people and systems, that has accepted responsibility to preserve information and make it available for one or more designated communities. May preserve data only and be assured to have the ability to read it. For some digital objects, this may be the best solution at least in the short-term because it ensures that the material is accessible by preserving the access tools as well as the object itself. However, various issues including space, maintenance, and costs may make this impossible in the longer term. Specifically, equipment ages and breaks, documentation disappears, vendor support vanishes, and the storage medium as well as the equipment deteriorates[6]

(k) Replication

Creating duplicate copies of data on one or more systems is called replication. Data that exists as a single copy in only one location is highly vulnerable to software or hardware failure, intentional or accidental alteration, and environmental catastrophes like fire, flooding, etc. Digital data is more likely to survive if it is replicated in several locations. Replicated data may introduce difficulties in refreshing, migration, versioning, and *access control* since the data is located in multiple places.

(l) Reliance on standards

Reliance to standards is mean to "harden" the encoding and formatting of digital objects by adhering to well-recognized standards and discarding proprietary or less-supported standards. It assumes in part that such standards will endure and that problems of compatibility resulting from the evolution of the computing environment (applications software, operating systems) will be handled by the continuing need to accommodate the standard within the new environment. Like many of the strategies described here, reliance on standards may lessen the immediate threat to a digital document from obsolescence, but it is no more a permanent preservation solution than the use of gold CDs or stone tablets.

(m) Normalisation

Normalization is a formalized implementation of reliance on standards. Within an archival repository, all digital objects of a particular type (e.g., colour images, structured text) are converted into a single chosen file format that is thought to embody the best overall compromise amongst characteristics such as functionality, longevity, and preservability. The Merits and disMerits of reliance on standards also apply to normalization.

(n) Universal Virtual Computer

Universal Virtual Computer is a form of emulation. It requires the development of a computer program independent of any existing hardware or software that could simulate the basic architecture of every computer since the beginning, including memory, a sequence of registers, and rules for how to move information among them. Users could create and save digital files using the application software of their choice, but all files would also be backed up in a way that could be read by the universal computer. To read the file in the future would require only a single emulation layer— between the universal virtual computer and the computer of that time

(o) Hardware Museum

Collect hardware and software from different generations to enable data to be accessed in its original environment.

Merits

- Data can be read on original devices and with original software.
- Older software (if available) can be installed and used.
- Obsolete formats can be read.

Demerits

- Not a solution for permanent preservation of data
- Difficult maintenance of old machines due to lack of replacement parts
- Knowledge of how to operate hardware and software components required. Relatively costly and expensive.

(p) Metadata Attachment

Metadata is data on a digital file that includes information on creation, access rights, restrictions, preservation history, and rights management.[7] Metadata attached to digital files may be affected by file format obsolescence. ASCII is considered to be the most durable format for metadata[8] because it is widespread, backwards compatible when used with Unicode, and utilizes human-readable characters, not numeric codes. It retains information, but not the structure information it is presented in. For higher functionality, SGML or XML should be used. Both markup languages are stored in ASCII format, but contain tags that denote structure and format.

(q) The Digital Tablet

Kranch proposes developing a digital tablet for preservation. The digital tablet technique does not precisely fit into the above categories. The tablet would have a self-contained power source, present the stored digital information on a screen as glyphs from a written language appropriate for the information, and have touch-sensitive controls to change the presentation and manipulate the information. Additionally, it should be able to withstand millennia of neglect under harsh conditions yet cost no more than a few dollars to produce and encode. It should have a storage capacity of dozens or hundreds of terabytes, and contain a simple serial read-only port to download the original digital information into an external system along with instructions on how to do it. However, the digital tablet may be considered to be another technology preservation method.

CONCLUSION

Books, manuscripts, are decaying. Some of them are still useful, but the damage is beyond restoration. To preserve their information contents it is urgently needed to digitize them. The aim of digital preservation is long-term, error-free storage of digital information, with the means of retrieval and interpretation, for the period of time that information is required. Preservation in the digital world is a challenging task for librarians. Digital libraries can serve as powerful tools for libraries to reach out to, expand their sphere of influence and strengthen their roles in the society. Several approaches for digital preservation have been identified and presented in this new era. Conventional methods are mainly technology emulation, information migration, and encapsulation [9, 10]. However, there is a lack of proven preservation methods to ensure that the information will continue to be readable. Digital preservation is a cost-intensive activity of continuing nature. The necessary financial and technological commitments to maintain digital contents and to migrate it to future generations must be an organizational commitment.

REFERENCES

1. Van der Hoeven, Jeffrey, Bram Lohman, and Verdegem, Remco (2007). Emulation for Digital Preservation in Practice: The Results. International Journal of Digital Curation, 2, no. 2. 123-132.
2. Day, Michael (2006). The long-term preservation of Web content. Berlin: Springer, 177-199.
3. Kapoor, Teena. Digital Preservation: Planning, Process and

Approaches for Libraries. Noida: Jaypee Institute of Information Technology.

4. Miguel J, Ferreira. A. (2007). Digital Preservation Challenge. Portugal: Department of Information Systems University of Minho..

5. Boudrez, Filip (2016). Digital containers for shipment into the future. Accessed January 21, 2016. http://www.expertise centrumdavid.be/docs/digital_containers.pdf

6. P. S. Graham (1993). Intellectual Preservation in the Electronic Environment. After the Electronic Revolution, Will You Be the First to Go?. Chicago: American Library Association.

7. NISO (2007). Framework Advisory Group. A Framework of Guidance for Building Good Digital Collections. Baltimore: NISO Framework Working Group..

8. National Initiative for a Networked Cultural Heritage. NINCH(2002). Guide to Good Practice in the Digital Representation and Management of Cultural Heritage Materials. Glascow: Humanities Advanced Technology and Information Institute.

9. Chen, S S.(2001).The Paradox of Digital Preservation. IEEE Computer 34, no. 3, 24-28.

10. Garrett J, and Waters D (1996). Preserving Digital Information, Report of the Task Force on Archiving of Digital Information. Washington: The Commission on Preservation and Access and The Research Libraries Group.

3

Digital Preservation: Planning, Strategies and Trends

Rajesh Kumar Singh*

ABSTRACT

Digital preservation is currently a major challenge for the information management, technological and scientific communities in all domains. It is also crucial at the organisational level with special pressure for all institutions with a responsibility for preservation, such as libraries and archives. Digital preservation is a very important part of the creation and management of any digital collection. Without the proper preservation a digital collection can easily become inaccessible and therefore useless in just a matter of a few years. Terms such as medium preservation and technology preservation are widely used when discussing issues related to the preservation of electronic records.

This paper discusses long-term archiving and long-term access to digital documents, with an emphasis on strategy for preservation. Selecting materials for digital preservation depends on whether the materials are both valuable and

* Deputy Librarian, Banaras Hindu University,Varanasi

endangered, whether appropriate digitization procedures and standards for these materials exist, and whether copyright allows reasonable access for educational and research purposes.

Keywords: Digital information, Preservation Planning, Digital archiving, Digital preservation, LOCKSS, Preservation Strategy, E-resources.

INTRODUCTION

'Digital' and 'Preservation' are two terms that encompass wide areas of interest in information management. The digital "factor" changes the nature of content, its forms of representation, media and usage; having deep implications for preservation. Preservation has long been one of the core functions of libraries and archives. It can be examined at two major levels: issues of meaningful collection and maintenance of content and, in a more strict sense, aspects of stability of the media that support such content.

A digital preservation strategy is a well-measured and documented approach to the preservation of digital items. For collecting archivists, the purpose of such an approach is to make sure that access to the born-digital archives accessioned by a repository can be maintained indefinitely (Helen H., 2006). For repositories responsible for personal digital archives this will probably include material created on long-past, recent, current and future computers and devices. This is a major challenge for digital archivists because the technological landscape evolves so rapidly: new hardware, software and removable media are developed and adopted on a regular basis, and new versions often only have limited backwards compatibility. Obsolescence therefore poses a major threat to the survival of digital records and must be addressed in a preservation strategy.

Digital archivists must also be able to demonstrate to user that a preserved digital object is authentic: that no accidental or intentional changes have occurred; and that the stated date of creation or receipt, identity of the author and process that created the object is all verifiable. Preservation strategies are all based on the principle that the preserved digital object should be identical in all essential respects to the digital object which left the creator's computer or other device (Kirchhoff, A. J., 2008). This means that it is important to understand what is 'essential' in order to protect those aspects of a record which are essential and to measure the success of preservation interventions.

DIGITAL PRESERVATION

Preservation for posterity has always been one of the main responsibilities of libraries. Traditional preservation has been an extension of the custodial function, under which importance was given to preservation of the 'physical form' – manuscripts, books, sculptures, gramophone records, etc. In the digital world, traditional preservation concept is undergoing a transformation, due to the special features of digital resources.

The UK CEDAR project has given the following definition of 'digital preservation': "Storage, maintenance and access to a digital object over the long term, usually as a consequence of applying one or more preservation strategies." (Digital Preservation coalition, 2002).

Digital documents are created using computer systems, and depend on them for con inued access. Hardware and software systems become outdated very rapidly, leading to technological obsolescence. Digital preservation, therefore, involves taking measures to ensure that the digital documents will remain available, usable and authentic in the future when the applications and systems, which were used to create and interpret them, might no longer are available.

Preservation of digital resources is much more complex than that of non-digital material such as paper. For example, when a book is preserved, all aspects of the book are preserved – its physical presence, format, layout and contents, since all these individual elements are inextricably linked. Digital formats on the other hand can be easily separated into individual elements; hence more efforts are needed to preserve them as a whole. For example, one can retain the content of the digital document while losing the layout (converting HTML to PDF format); or one can maintain its physical presence i.e. the computer file, but fail to preserve its readability. One can think of the following different levels at which digital resources can be preserved:

Preserve the physical presence : Also known as 'bit preservation', under which the computer file is preserved.

Preserve the content : Since actual information content is the most crucial component, one can provide access to it at its lowest level such as ASCII text, without the add-ons such as font variations or layout features.

Preserve the presentation : The original format or layout may include different font faces and sizes, columns, margins, the use of white space etc. that carry out functions such as emphasizing important parts of the text, improving clarity, etc. In many formats of digital documents (e.g. SGML, XML), the layout specifications are separate from the content. To maintain the original look of the document, these layout specifications must also be preserved.

Preserve the functionality : Special efforts are required to preserve the functionality of digital documents, which might contain multimedia components, exist in hypertext format and have navigation functions such as toolbars, keyword search or interactive tables of contents.

Digital preservation is the series of actions and interventions required to ensure continued and reliable access to authentic digital objects for as long as they are deemed to be of value (McDonald J. and Van de Velde, E., 2004).

In order to preserve materials on a scale commensurate with mass storage capabilities and in formats that are accessible and usable, it is necessary to articulate some basic requirements.

User's perspective : User's expectation is always changing, yet users, especially research scholars need both traditional documents and electronic documents of old information and current information.

Institutions's responsibility : Libraries, archives and other custodians have responsibility for their any properties. So institutions should plan for digital materials including their maintenance, preservation and distribution.

Mission of parent institution : First object of libraries, archives and other custodians is to satisfy the user's expectation and user's requirements. They should preserve all materials in all formats.

Storage media : Storage media is having different formats such as text, data graphics, video and sound, different storage capacity like floppy disk, CD-ROM (R/R-W), DVD ROM (R/R-W), Pen drive, External Hard disk drive etc.(Beagrie, N. and Jones, M., 2002).

SELECTION FOR PRESERVATION

"Selection" is another important issue in digital preservation. The huge quantity of information being produced digitally, its variable quality, and the resource constraints on those taking responsibility to preserve long-term access make selectivity unavoidable for archiving.

Traditionally, lack of selection for preservation may not necessarily mean that the item will be lost, but in the digital environment non-selection for preservation will almost surely mean loss of the item. Although not all resources need to be preserved forever, some will not need to be preserved at all, others will need to be preserved only for a defined period of time, and a relatively small sub-set will need to be preserved indefinitely. Selecting materials for digital preservation depends on three criteria:

- Whether the materials are both valuable and endangered;
- Whether appropriate digitization procedures and standards for these materials exist;
- Whether copyright allows reasonable access for educational and research purposes.

However, just as the web allows anyone to publish information on it without having to obtain any formal permission, it also allows its removal. The library must capture relevant free as well as paid web-based resources whenever they are available, in order to safeguard against their possible loss from the web, so that they can provide continued access to these resources to its users (Obaiah, B. and J., Francis, 2008). Though libraries will have to cater to remote access to resources (online journals, online full-text databases etc.) as a part of collection development, it would be desirable to download and preserve selected core resources on local servers.

DEGREE OF PRESERVATION

A digital object, such as the kind of typical object found in a personal archive (e.g. a speech written in a word-processed document, a budget in a spreadsheet, or a digital image of a family) is defined in the PREMIS Data Dictionary as a discrete unit of information in digital form which is comprised of three different levels:

Bit stream : in its simplest form, a digital object consists of a bit stream, i.e. an ordered sequence of bits (binary zeros and ones). This binary inscription will usually be stored on a physical medium of some kind. A computer system with the correct combination of hardware or software translates the bitstream into something meaningful.

File : a named and ordered sequence of bytes known by an operating system. The format of a file is laid out in the format specification, which transforms the file from its binary ones and zeros into something which makes sense to a user, i.e. stipulating the proper encoding, sequence, arrangement, size and internal relationships which enable the construction of a valid file of the relevant type (e.g. jpeg 2013 a file). This level represents the transformation of the input bit stream into output for presentation purposes; the physical medium on which the bit stream is inscribed is therefore of no consequence at this level.

Representation : denotes the set of files needed for a complete and reasonable rendition of an Intellectual Entity. This is defined by PREMIS as a coherent set of content that can reasonably be described as a unit; this is essentially a conceptual object, or something that a human can understand as a meaningful unit of information, e.g. a website, a report, a photograph. An Intellectual Entity or conceptual object may have one or more digital representations or encodings; for instance, the text of a politician's speech might be saved as both a Microsoft Word document and a PDF file. The underlying encoding of each will differ considerably, but the textual content of each item is identical.

Simply preserving the bit stream therefore does not guarantee ongoing access to a digital object. The digital object has an existence separate from the medium on which the bit stream is inscribed and successful preservation is only complete when all the significant properties are maintained and the digital object can be displayed in a meaningful and understandable form. In some cases, this might mean that only the intellectual content (e.g. the text of a word-processed document) is preserved, and that original formatting and layout is not retained in the preserved object. However, in other cases (notably, but not exclusively, complex objects such as interactive resources) it may be important that the 'look and feel' of the original object, and its functionality, is retained or recreated as part of the preservation process.

INTEGRATING DIGITAL PRESERVATION IN LIBRARY

Long-term preservation is an important mission for a digital preservation system in a library. It ensures that the digital collection the library builds will be preserved for future users, regardless of the vagaries of institutional funding and decisions made by publishers (Rebecca, P., 2013). However, that is only half of the story. Unless users can access preserved content when it is no longer available from the publishers, it is like locking print media in a sealed vault with no key for safekeeping. The content might be safe, but it is certainly not useful.

MISSION

The other mission for a library's digital preservation system is to make the preserved content available whenever it is needed. That may occur at any time for one of many reasons: there could be a temporary interruption of internet access, the publisher may have blocked access to the library because of a mistake or a dispute, or the library may simply have canceled their subscription and permanently lost access. Regardless of the reason, the digital preservation system must be ready immediately to serve its content in place of the publisher's.

STRATEGY/TECHNIQUES

A digital preservation strategy is a well-considered and

documented approach to the preservation of digital objects. For collecting archivists, the purpose of such a strategy is to ensure that access to the born-digital archives accessioned by a repository can be maintained indefinitely. For repositories responsible for personal digital archives this will probably include material created on long-past, recent, current and future computers and devices. This is a major challenge for digital archivists because the technological landscape evolves so rapidly: new hardware, software and removable media are developed and adopted on a regular basis, and new versions often only have limited backwards compatibility. Obsolescence therefore poses a major threat to the survival of digital records and must be addressed in a preservation strategy.

Different strategies are being used to carry out preservation of digital resources. Some of the significant ones are:

Migration : Under this method, there is a periodic transfer of digital materials from one hardware/software configuration to another. For example, file formats are converted into compatible new formats as soon as the original formats face the risk of becoming obsolete (e.g., HTML 3.2 to HTML 4.02 or .doc to .docx)

Emulation : It involves retaining information about how a digital object was created and accessed so that future access can be accurately and authentically reproduced. Emulation retains the functionality, look and feel of the original document.

Technology Preservation : This involves preservation of the technical environment by conserving the software and hardware needed for interpreting digital information.

Conversion of data to standardized format : Data could be transferred to ASCII format. It retains information, but not the structure or functionality.

Universal Virtual Computer (UVC) : One of the latest techniques to be explored is the UVC-based preservation method, which allows digital objects to be reconstructed in its original appearance anytime in the future, a programme or emulator is written to carry out this interpretation in the machine language of the UVC at the time the record was archived (without requiring any knowledge of the future target machine). The data can be stores in any format and the knowledge required to decode it is encapsulated in the UVC programme (format decoder). The UVC concept consists of the UVC itself, a logical data scheme with type description, the UVC programme and the logical data viewer.

FILE FORMATS SELECTION FOR DIGITAL PRESERVATION

File formats encode information into forms that can only be processed and rendered comprehensible by very specific combinations of hardware and software. The accessibility of that information is therefore highly vulnerable in today's rapidly evolving technological environment. This issue is not solely the concern of digital archivists, but of all those responsible for managing and sustaining access to electronic records over even relatively short timescales.

According to Lavoie, Issues to consider when selecting file formats for long-term preservation include:

- Is it defined by an international, national or publicly available standard?
- Is the quality of the specification adequate?
- How widely has the format been adopted as a preservation format?
- Is it backwards compatible?
- Is it independent of any specific hardware or software environment?
- Does it have good metadata support (i.e. metadata providing technical and provenance information which is generated by the creating application, entered manually by the record creator, or a combination of these)?
- Does it have a good range of functionality without being too complex for the purpose?
- Is it easily convertible into other formats (for migration purposes)?
- How well does it retain the formatting and other significant properties of converted digital objects?
- How stable is the format?

- How proven is it in terms of longevity?
- Does it include an error-detection facility? (Lavoie B., 2004).

One other approach to selecting preservation formats is provided by OCLC's INFORM Methodology, which measures the preservation durability of digital formats. It compares formats and preservation approaches, and provides a risk management-based means of tracking what might be lost over time if particular preservation actions are taken; the digital archivist can then make decisions about preservation strategy based on this risk assessment (Reich, V. and Rosenthal, D., 2001).

If a digital repository chooses to convert digital objects to one or more standard formats, there are a number of ways for consideration; examples for text-based documents include:

Extensible Markup Language (XML) : this is not a format, rather a general-purpose markup language for describing the structure and meaning of data. It is an open standard defined by the World Wide Web Consortium and is independent of specific applications. Preserving digital objects which have been created using XML in accordance with a standard DTD or Schema is straightforward. Converting other digital objects to XML is one kind of migration approach but with its own limitations.

OASIS Open Document Format for Office Applications: this is an open, XML-based, format for office files, such as word-processed documents or spreadsheets. It has been adopted as an international standard (ISO/IEC 26300) and offers a suitable format for the preservation of digital documents created in proprietary office formats like those generated by Microsoft Office.

Portable Document Format Archive (PDF/A) : this is a constrained version of Adobe's PDF version 1.4 which has been adopted as an international standard (ISO 19005-1). It is preservation-friendly. Its specification is openly available. It eliminates elements likely to complicate decoding and accelerate obsolescence (e.g. audio and video elements, or encryption, etc., which are sometimes used in other PDF formats); it is self-contained (i.e. can be displayed without any reliance on information from external sources); and support for embedding metadata is very good. Records saved to this format have a look and feel which is fundamentally one of text and images designed to fit a particular page size. However, it preserves static visual appearance only, so it is not suited in cases where functionality or logical structure needs to be preserved.

FOR IMAGES INCLUDE THE FOLLOWING ELEMENTS

Tagged Image File Format (TIFF) : a format used for raster (i.e. pixel-based) images. It is widely adopted and supported by most image processing and viewing applications, and it supports sophisticated colour management features. Many repositories consider TIFF to be the best option for preserving images, and it is often used to store archival masters of digitised images.

Joint Photographic Experts Group (JPEG) : a widely used format to represent continuous tone images (e.g. photographs and grey scale images). It is defined by an international standard (ISO 10918).

There are also widely accepted options for sound formats (e.g. WAVE LPCM or MP3_FF) and moving image formats (e.g. MPEG-2, MPEG-4_AVC). Many digital repositories publish details of the preservation formats they support, where more information about accepted formats can be found.

An important consideration when selecting a preservation format is how successfully the chosen format embodies the essential attributes, or significant properties, of the original digital object.

COMPARISON OF SIX MAJOR E-JOURNAL ARCHIVING PROGRAMMES

The following six programmes have been selected for comparative study. They are operated by organisations with excellent credentials in this field. At this early stage and given the varied factors which need to be taken into account to meet the needs of individual institutions, none completely deal with all requirements. It may be helpful to see the different features, pros and cons of these e-journal archiving programmes to choose a better one.

(a) LOCKSS

LOCKSS (Lots of Copies Keep Stuff Safe) enables participating libraries to collect, store, preserve and provide access to their own local copies of content to which they have subscribed. The LOCKSS system was one of the two very different e-journal archiving approaches (the other being what is now known as Portico) supported by the Mellon Foundation in 2002. The LOCKSS application is open-source software. LOCKSS enables members to harvest the web-based presentation files of the content of e-journals to which they have subscribed from participating publishers. Access is triggered whenever (and for whatever reason) the material cannot be viewed on the publisher's (or intermediary's) servers. The highly distributed nature of the approach aims to ensure that there is sufficient replication to safeguard content despite any potential disasters which might be fall individual LOCKSS institutions. LOCKSS introduced the LOCKSS Alliance as a membership organization in 2005 to introduce governance to the program and address sustainability issues. In 2006, the JISC funded a two-year initiative, including a UK support post, to raise awareness of LOCKSS. A total of 24 institutions from around the UK joined the initiative, with a further 6 funding their own participation in the trial (Stanford University, LOCKSS Programme, 2013).

Pros

- It allows libraries to collect and exert control over the material they licence, as they have done when purchasing print journals.
- LOCKSS has increased publisher participation and the number of titles at a great rate.
- It covers a significant number of smaller and therefore probably more vulnerable publishers.
- It requires relatively modest investment in staff and equipment.
- It permits immediate access to the archive whenever there is a problem with communication with a publisher's server, even if very short term.

Cons

- It will need ongoing technical support.
- Although much technical support is managed remotely, staff from the subscribing institution needs to monitor the local server and ensure that it is running correctly.
- Future software development will require an active LOCKSS developer community.
- It may be difficult to integrate with other institutional technical platforms, e.g. several UK LOCKSS pilot reports referred to difficulties of proxy integration, though only one appeared to think this would be a major barrier.
- Neither all titles of a particular publisher, nor all issues of a particular title are necessarily included in the LOCKSS collection.
- The larger STM publishers such as Elsevier have not demonstrated an enthusiasm for joining, and have expressed some concern about security of licensed content when it is distributed so widely. The resulting lack of major publisher content was a concern raised by several LOCKSS participants in their reports.

(b) CLOCKSS

CLOCKSS "Controlled LOCKSS" was launched in 2006 and is still at a relatively early stage of development. A not-for-profit collaboration between libraries and publishers, it is a dark archive based on the LOCKSS software in which a limited number of libraries take on an archival role on behalf of a broader community. CLOCKSS ingests and saves either source or a presentation file as the publisher chooses. Each library hosts two servers which create a network of dark repositories. CLOCKSS intends to add a limited number of additional libraries and more publishers in the next phase. It describes itself as complementary to LOCKSS, and a "strategic component in a multilayer, resilient, local and international preservation plan." The 7 libraries participating in CLOCKSS are also members of the LOCKSS Alliance, 6 are U.S Based, and one is in the UK (University of Edinburgh).

Pros

- It provides a community approach, with a small number of distributed libraries assuming responsibility for long-term archiving, working in partnership with publishers.
- Low cost. The CLOCKSS website claims that "Fees are low and for a limited period while we build the CLOCKSS Endowment which we expect to underwrite costs after five years."
- It is likely to appeal to publishers with concerns about security of access and therefore attract a broader range of content from major publishers.

Cons

- Post-cancellation access is not supported.
- Long term costs are not clear, though there is an expressed commitment to reducing costs through the creation of an endowment.
- It is too early to be able to assess the long-term viability of the programme, including funding support.
- It is unclear what motivations (other than public good) CLOCKSS centres would have for continuing to participate in the programme long-term.

(c) Portico

Portico is the second approach to e-journal archiving supported by the Mellon Foundation. It was launched as an independent organisation in 2005, though it has been in planning and preparation since 2002 under the auspices of Ithaka and with support from JSTOR.

Designed specifically as a third party service for scholarly literature published in electronic form, beginning with e-journals, it provides insurance to libraries that the e-journal content they have subscribed to will be preserved for the long-term. Portico provides access to the participating publisher is able to provide, Portico preserves normalised source files and/ or presentation files of e-journals and also performs interpretation archiving. If no presentation files are provided,

Portico creates new presentation files. Portico can become a delivery mechanism in the event of a trigger event. In addition, if a publisher has designated Portico as such, it can also serve as a potential mechanism for post cancellation access.

Pros

- It removes the onus of managing the content from the library and provides assurance of long-term preservation.
- It can also provide post cancellation access providing the publisher has nominated them as a potential mechanism for this.
- Publisher participation has grown at an impressive rate. Some of the major STM publishers, such as Elsevier has joined.
- Their archiving approach is very thorough, preserving source files and/or presentation files, depending on what the publisher chooses to supply.
- The recent agreement with the KB to act as a mirror site for Portico strengthens their credibility.
- It provides an equitable business model, with publishers contributing to costs as well as libraries.

Cons

- Some see the dependence on publishers for revenue as a weakness.
- The fees libraries pay to Portico may be higher than other options.
- The current focus seems to be on the larger publishers Like CLOCKSS; it requires a cultural shift from libraries in terms of their traditional custodial role.
- Some believe that the title and publisher coverage could become rather US-centric once major international publishers have been covered.

(d) e-Depot

The Koninklijke Bibliotheek (KB) is the national library of the Netherlands and operates e- Depot, its archive for the Dutch national deposit collection of electronic publications and other e-content (e.g. Dutch newspapers). e-Depot, which is OAIS compliant, was established in 2003 and focused initially on Dutch material. Recognising the international nature of journal publishing, this has now been extended to international publications. The KB intends to conclude archiving agreements for all the journals from 20-25 of the world's largest publishers. Publishers wishing to make use of the services provided by e-Depot are required to conclude an archiving agreement with the KB and to deliver bulk content and specified metadata. The primary deposit file format is PDF. Generally, end-user access is restricted to on-site perusal for reasons of private research only and on-line access is denied.

KB, who is committed to a programme of research and development in this area, is promoting the concept of the "Safe Places Network". This recognises the power and utility of international cooperation in finding solutions to the challenges of long-term preservation. A recent example is the decision by Portico to lodge a copy of their archive with KB.

Pros

- e-Depot aims to cover all major STM publishers. It already has more than 12 major publishers on board.
- The KB has a strong reputation for leadership in digital preservation research and practice.
- e-Depot saves both rendition and source files.
- There are no costs involved for others; the service is currently underwritten by the Dutch government. KB sales literature though includes the statement "In the coming years the KB intends to develop a sustainable business model for the e-Depot which will reflect both the public and private responsibility for our digital and cultural heritage."
- They have demonstrated a good understanding of technical issues.

Cons

- Because they are such major publishers, the trigger events which could provide open access to content archived by e-Depot are highly unlikely to occur.
- It is extremely doubtful that the KB will want to engage in managing numerous authentication systems in the case of cancellation of content, the trigger event most likely to cause disruption for most organisations licensing access.
- At the moment, assured access is only available onsite at the KB.

(e) Electronic Collections Online (ECO)

ECO was launched by OCLC in 1997 as a subscription service for libraries to a wide range of e-journals. It currently provides web access through OCLC's First Search service to over 5,000 titles from over 40 publishers. OCLC negotiates with publishers for perpetual access rights for subscribers to the service and for it to migrate back files to new formats if required.

Pros

- The emphasis is on continued access, which is likely to be of paramount concern to most libraries.
- It has been in operation longer than any of the others.
- It has a significant number of publishers and titles and good content coverage.

Cons

- Continued access is dependent on payment of an access fee. If titles are cancelled, access to past content can only be resumed if a subscription is reinstated within a five year period.
- ECO is primarily a tailored aggregator service for libraries: long term preservation is not their main mission.
- The emphasis on current access may be detrimental to long-term preservation (though some libraries find this feature makes the service easier to justify funding).

(f) British Library e-journal Digital Archive

Over the past few years the BL has been building a Digital Object Management System (DOM) capable of storing and managing all digital content the BL takes responsibility for, including their own digitally created content, material purchased and material acquired through voluntary and legal deposit. The DOM system, which will be OAIS16 compliant, has three geographically dispersed identical nodes to provide redundancy in the event of loss of data from any one node.

The BL is currently assessing the feasibility of providing archiving and preservation solutions over and above those envisaged for e-legal deposit. The British Library began ingesting content from selected publishers during 2007, but is still finalising the exact service options that will be provided.

Access will depend on publishers' requirements. BL proposes two levels of service, Grey Archive (BL Reading Room access only), and Light Archive with content made available on the Internet worldwide following a publisher-specified trigger event (Maniatis, Petros and others, 2005).

Pros

- The British Library's strong reputation, experience and mandate for preservation generally;
- The archive is funded by charges to publishers and there are no other costs for libraries;
- The BL's extensive planning and preparation for digital deposit in building an infrastructure capable of dealing with both volume and complexity of material.

Cons

- It is too early to assess the content they will attract. As yet there is no detail of which publishers are on board. The emphasis is on recruiting publisher participation.
- The trigger events the BL use do not include post-cancellation access (apart from BL Reading Room access).

CRITERIA FOR JUDGING RELEVANCE AND VALUE OF NEW ARCHIVING INITIATIVES

Factors which might impact on decision making for

archiving solutions could include:

- Does the service include titles which are core to our institution's primary clientele/designated community?
- Does the overall bundle of titles in the archive meet our needs?
- Is our Library planning a move to e-only access?
- Does our Library intend to deselect print journals as electronic back files become available?
- Do we need assurance of continued online access?
- Do we need assurance of continued access for an indefinite period/longer than 10 years?
- Can we afford the service and does it represent value for money?

If the answer is yes to most of the above, then it will certainly be worthwhile investing in a trusted archiving solution, such as LOCKSS, Portico, and/or CLOCKSS.

Assuming the title is covered in more than one archive, what factors might affect which solution to go for?

- Do we want control over the titles that we have subscribed to in a similar way to print?
- Do we need seamless access following a trigger event?
- Do we want to delegate responsibilitv for archiving and perpetual access to a trusted third party?(e.g. Portico)
- Are we more concerned about the vulnerability of titles from smaller publishing houses rather than the major players?

If there is a combination of the content being of key importance and concern about the early stage of archiving solutions, it could be advisable to subscribe to more than one; assuming the content of primary interest is offered.

SELECTING THE RIGHT PRESERVATION STRATEGY

There are various theories on the best way to preserve digital material, and a number of different approaches have been developed, which in turn have variants. They range from preserving the original technology on which the archival digital objects ran, to preserving only the significant properties of an object, which are defined independently of any specific hardware or software platform. Each approach has advantages and disadvantages.

Thibodeau suggests that a digital archive should take the following four criteria into consideration when selecting a preservation strategy:

Feasibility : possession of hardware and software capable of implementing the chosen method.

Sustainability : the method should be capable of being applied indefinitely into the future; or there should be another path which will offer a sequel to the method if it ceases being sustainable.

Practicality : implementation should be within reasonable limits of difficulty and expense.

Appropriateness : the chosen approach should be appropriate for the particular types of digital objects to be preserved and the objectives of their preservation.

Some preservation methods only apply to specific hardware or software platforms, some to individual data types or formats, while others are very general. Depending on the range and variety of digital objects to be preserved by a repository, selection of approach might be limited to methods that are optimal for this range, or (if very wide ranging) a method with broad applicability should be chosen.

CONCLUSION

The problem of long-term digital preservation is becoming more real in the midst of a digital era. Old assumptions regarding information preservation are no longer valid, and it is clear that aggressive actions are needed to ensure the understandability of data for ages to come. In order to address these challenges, new technologies and systems are being developed. Such systems will be able to better address these vital issues if they are equipped with storage technology that is inherently dedicated to preservation and that supports the different aspects of the preservation environment. An appropriate storage system will make any solution more robust and lower the probability of data corruption or loss.

Although there is a trend towards "e-only" options, restraining factors include some academics distrust of e-publications and resistance to change. Drivers for a move to e-only include access, space, user expectations, and round the clock availability. It would be helpful if a cost-benefit analysis could be carried out comparing the savings from hardcopy cancellations (space, binding etc) with e-only licensing plus archiving costs. Which solution, if any, is chosen will depend on several factors including critical mass of content, numbers of publishers, numbers of titles, issue coverage, and costs. It should be acknowledged that publishers themselves may be able and willing to provide ongoing post-cancellation access, though this may be a chargeable service.

With the Digital Millennium Act in force, the publishers are not obligated to provide perpetual online access to content to which libraries used to have subscription. Implementing the LOCKSS/CLOCKSS concept in library can facilitate the perpetual access to such content. This, of course, can be done only through negotiation with the concerned publisher and it is likely to have financial implications.

Despite these agreements and developments, the field of digital archiving is still in its infancy, and much work needs to be accomplished to achieve a secure and permanent archiving of electronic journals.

Our study has examined different approaches to archiving and preservation. All deserve support and encouragement, but none currently offers the typical academic library a complete solution to their archival needs. Nor do any of them currently cover the greater proportion of the journal titles being published today.

REFERENCES

1. Beagrie, N. and Jones, M. (2002). Trusted Digital Repositories: Attributes and Responsibilities. Mountain View, CA, Research Libraries Group- OCLC, available at ***http://www.rlg.org/longterm/repositories.pdf***
2. "CLOCKSS (2014). *http://www.clockss.org* (Accessed on 18

October 2014).

3. Digital Millennium **Act (2014).** available at *http://www.copyright.gov.in.legislation/dmca.pdf* (Accessed on 18 October 2014).

4. Digital Preservation Coalition **(2002).** Preservation Management of Digital Materials: A Handbook. Digital Preservation Coalition, New York. Available at *www.dpconline.org/graphics/handbook/* (Accessed on 22 October 2014).

5. Hockx-Yu, Helen (2006). Digital preservation in the context of institutional repositories. Electronic library and information systems. Vol. 40, No. 3, pp. 232-243.

6. Kirchhoff, Amy J. (2008). Digital preservation: challenges and implementation. Learned Publishing, 21, pp. 285–294.

7. Lavoie, B. (2004). The Incentives to Preserve Digital Materials: Roles, Scenarios, and Economic Decision-Making. White Paper, OCLC Research, available at: *www.oclc.org/research/projects/digipres/incentives-dp.pdf* (Accessed on 22 October 2014).

8. LOCKSS(2014)., Wikipedia, available at *http://en.wikipedia.org/wiki/LOCKSS* (Accessed on 18 October 2014).

9. Maniatis, Petros [et al]. (2005). The LOCKSS Peer-to-Peer Digital Preservation System. ACM Transactions on Computer Systems, 23, Issue 1, pp. 2–50.

10. McDonald, J. and Van de Velde, E. (2004). The lure of linking. Library Journal, available at: *www.libraryjournal.com/article/CA405398.html* (Accessed on 08 October 2014).

11. Obaiah, B. and Jayakanth, Francis (2008).Long-term preservation and perpetual access to scholarly content: the LOCKSS way. Proceedings of National conference on digitization and digital preservation, pp. 190-194.

12. Pool, Rebecca (2013). Mind the gap: catching digital content before it slips away - PRESERVATION- Research Information. available at *www.researchinformation.info/features/feature.php?feature_id=397* (Accessed on 16 October 2014).

13. Reich, V. and Rosenthal, D. (2001). LOCKSS: a permanent Web publishing and access system." D-LIB Magazine, Vol. 7, No. 6. Available at: *www.dlib.org/dlib/june01/reich/06reich.html* (Accessed on 25 October 2014).

14. Rosenthal, David S. H.; Lipkis, Thomas Robertson; Thomas S. and Morabito, Seth (2005). Transparent Format Migration of

Preserved Web Content. D-Lib Magazine (Corporation for National Research Initiatives) 11 (1). doi:10.1045/january2005-rosenthal. (Accessed on 25 October 2014).

15. Stanford University LOCKSS Program (2013). LOCKSS: Lots of Copies Keep Stuff Safe, Stanford University, Stanford. available at: *www.lockss.org* (Accessed on 15 October 2014).

16. *http://www.paradigm.ac.uk/workbook/preservation-strategies/* (Accessed on 25 October 2014).

17. *http://www.nationalarchives.gov.uk/documents/selecting-file-formats.pdf* (Accessed on 25 October 2014).

18. *https://www.jisccollections.ac.uk/Documents/e_journal_archiving_%20solutions_comparative_study.pdf* (Accessed on 25 October 2014).

19. *http://www.clir.org/PUBS/reports/pub107/pub107.pdf* (Accessed on 25 October 2014).

4

Guidelines for Digital Preservation Policy

K. Nazeer Badhusha*

ABSTRACT

The difficulty and expense of preserving digital information is a potential impediment to digital library development. Preservation of traditional materials became more successful and systematic after libraries and archives integrated preservation into overall planning and resource allocation. Digital preservation is largely experimental and replete with the risks associated with untested methods. Digital preservation strategies are shaped by the needs and constraints of repositories with little consideration for the requirements of current and future users of digital scholarly resources. This article discusses the present state of digital preservation policy, articulates requirements of both users and custodians, and suggests research needs in storage media, migration, conversion, and overall management strategies. Additional research in these areas would help developers of digital libraries and other institutions with preservation responsibilities to integrate long-term preservation into program planning, administration, system architectures, and resource allocation.

* Chief Librarian, Hindustan Institute of Engineering Technology, Chennai, Tamilnadu

Keywords : Digital Library, Digital Collection, Digital Preservation

INTRODUCTION

This tool examines policies in use for preserving and maintaining digital materials and ensuring their availability for current and future use. in particular, it dwells upon some specific aspects such as costs, requirements, roles, responsibilities, monitoring and review etc.

A policy forms the pillar of a programme for digital preservation. It gives general direction for the whole of an organization, and as such it remains on a reasonably high level. Actual steps in implementing a preservation programme have to be in accordance with the policy in order to guarantee their coherence. From an external point of view, a written policy is a sign that the organization takes the responsibility to preserve digital material.

At the present time, the policies for ensuring long-term storage, maintenance, migration and access to digital materials, whether at the local or national level, are not frequently present both in the private and in the public sectors. Moreover, the policies publicly available via web are mainly developed by cultural heritage institutions and have been elaborated very recently.

Frequently, the confusion about the most appropriate practices and methods, the lack of a consensus, the difficulty in engaging the interest for these themes and the shortage of good models for digital preservation can be some of the difficulties that institutions meet in developing their policies, even if the need for defining policies is increasing at the same degree of the growth of the digital heritage.

The primary aims of a policy are to be provided guidance and authorization on the preservation of digital materials and to ensure the authenticity, reliability and long-term accessibility of them. Moreover, a policy should explain how digital preservation can serve major needs of an institution and state some principles and rules on specific aspects which then laid the basis of implementation.

This tool sets out to identify and describe the reasons that have induced an institution to develop its policy for digital preservation, the advantages of having it, the definite areas that are included in it, the most important problems discussed and other specific and relevant aspects, as those above-mentioned.

GENERAL PRINCIPLES

Some general principles should be followed for qualifying this activity:

- a policy needs to convey the very philosophy of an organization concerning digital preservation. it should induce a common understanding of the objectives, of whether each collection item should be preserved with maximum effort possibly applying multiple preservation paths, or whether a certain pragmatism should be pursued.
- a digital policy should facilitate the sustainability of an institution's present and future digital holdings.
- a digital preservation policy has to demonstrate its benefits, its effectiveness.
- a digital policy should be connected and integrated with a risk assessment document.
- every policy should be practicable, not definitive, capable of being put into practice by institutions with varying resources and needs, and, especially, flexible to adapt itself to changing administrative and technological circumstances.
- any policy should be characterized by clarity, adequacy, transparency, efficiently, effectiveness and logical organization of contents.
- a digital preservation policy should be written in a simple and suitable language, without redundancies and, at the same time, without lowering the level of quality contained in its contents.
- once a digital preservation policy is operative, it should be re-though, reviewed or newly conceived on a regular basis to take into account changes in the organizational, legal and technical environment and to make rules and

guidelines more precise and explicit where there is any ambiguity about implementation.

- a digital policy should offer achievable solutions, provide for the management training and, finally, be maintained through time.

BENEFITS OF DIGITAL PRESERVATION

Table 1

Benefits	To develop a digital preservation strategy
	To plan coherent digital preservation programmes
	To ensure and reinforce accountability
	To demonstrate that such funds can and will be used responsibly and consistently
	To ensure digital materials available for current and future use
	To define the significant properties that need to be preserved for particular classes resources
	To assist agencies in designing digitisation programmes
	To provide a comprehensive statement on the digital preservation
	To provide security measures that ensure the protection of digital materials during use

A digital preservation policy could guarantee many benefits at each institutional level, such as ensuring digital materials available for current and future use, providing a comprehensive statement on this theme and planning coherent digital preservation programmes. Besides, the formulation of a policy allows to deal with difficult subjects as the short-lasting life span and small capacities of digital materials, the obsolescence of the hardware required to access them, the obsolescence of software for reading the data and file formats and, finally, the structural and technical heterogeneity of the different types of digital materials.

SCOPE AND OBJECTIVES

In according to an institution's achievable resources, the main scope of a digital preservation policy is to achieve the following objectives:

- preserving and providing continued access to digital material, both born digital and digitised material.
- ensuring that preserved digital materials are authentic.
- preserving damage and deterioration of the physical media by ensuring an environmental control.
- reversing damage, if it's possible.
- changing the format of digital materials to preserve their intellectual content, if it's necessary.

REQUIREMENTS

Table 2

Requirements	Legal requirements	
	Financial requirements	
	Business requirements	
	Technical requirements	Maintenance procedures
		Preservation strategies
		Technology forecasting
	Historical value	

The reasons behind the positioning of policy development for digital preservation within institutions are several and can vary according to the specific juridical and institutional contexts. in many cases, the political context in which a policy is formed weights heavily as well as the legal environment. Moreover, there are other relevant factors, such as the substantial financial requirements, the business requirements to take evidence of decisions and activities and ensure the historical value of digital materials. Technical requirements constitute another important reason for developing a policy, specifically as far as it concerns the definition of technology forecasting, maintenance procedures and, especially, preservation strategies, or rather the precise guidelines for reformatting, refreshing, migrating, emulating and bundling data to newer technological platforms.

ROLES AND RESPONSIBILITIES

A policy should identify the actors and assign

responsibilities for digital preservation, not by giving names but rather by outlining the overall organization and business structure. This may include outsourcing certain functions to external providers, or cooperation with an associated initiative in specific tasks. Furthermore, a policy should state the commitment to training the preservation staff and informing other actors. in particular, it should provide methods for increasing the level of staff expertise with digital preservation, such as local courses in computer or digital technology, training provided by professional organizations or by vendors, independent study or assessment, hire consultants and hire staff with digital knowledge or experience. People who has responsibility in the developing and implementation of a digital preservation policy should carry out the following functions:

- making decisions of retention, use and preservation of digital materials at the acquisition or creation stage, not later.
- establishing maintenance procedures and quality control within monitoring processes and programmes.
- establishing and implementing strategies for digital preservation, such as migration, emulation or technology preservation.
- developing a disaster recovery programme.
- ensuring security of access to digital materials.

CONTEXT

A digital policy can be part of a national/regional initiative or can be formulated and developed within each institution. In the first case, the policy will must respect and entirely apply all national/regional rules, regulations, standard and guidelines regarding preservation issues for digital materials. in the other case, it will represent the final result of a careful analysis conducted on institution's own initiative to solve internal problems concerning these themes. Another important question regards the integration of a policy in an existing business structure. it could be difficult and tricky in that digital preservation has a tight interaction with all stages in the information lifecycle and other segments of an organization.

Therefore, a digital preservation policy should commit to a smooth integration with other policies and business processes, by identifying and communicating possible interrelations and synergies.

COVERAGE AREAS

Table 3

Areas	Authority and responsibility
	Conversion and reformatting
	Appraisal, selection and acquisition
	Storage and maintenance
	Access and dissemination
	Implementation
	Standards
	Procedures
	Quality control, auditing and benchmarking
	Cooperation
	Technical infrastructure

A digital preservation policy should be structured in several specific and distinctive areas, such as those above-mentioned. It should be introduced by two sections, respectively the purpose and the scope of the policy, to better explain, show and clarify all the questions that will be then largely discussed in it. in particular, referring to the purpose, a digital preservation policy should view the mandate of the repository, possible external legal pressures, the value of the digital material and, finally, the expected use in the future. A special area should be dedicated to the cooperation between institutions in the policy process. usually, the cooperation regards archives, libraries, museums or other repositories can be local, national or even international and provides that the work and engagement can be distributed equally or in a different way between participant members. Furthermore, standards relevant to preservation are of great value as they facilitate cooperation and hold the knowledge and experience of other initiatives. therefore, a policy should include the intention to adhere to relevant standards.

Another important section concerns the responsibilities involved specifically with reference to the implementation and the related human resources and tools, such as management, employees, special task force, external advice, resources or models. in some cases, results of internal analyses, first of all risk analysis, are the main actors in the drawing up of the policy. Really, an accurate list of risks inherent in systems that preserve digital materials can help to formulate a more comprehensive policy on these themes. therefore, it is necessary to emphasize that a digital preservation policy should aim to minimize the risks associated with technological changes and allow for other changes. In this way, materials in digital form can be preserved and always remain comprehensible even if, for example, the organizational structure changes. Another area should be dedicated to benchmarking, in particular referring to measures of the access of the policy and audit.

COSTS

Table 4

Costs	Technical infrastructure	Equipment purchases, maintenance and upgrades
		Software/hardware obsolescence monitoring/ review
		Network connectivity
	Financial plan	Strategy and methods
		Commitment to long-term funding
	Staffing	Hiring training
	infrastructure	Ongoing training
	Outsourcing	

Costs carry on a primary role in the developing of digital preservation policies. in fact, factors such as outsourcing, financial plan, technical infrastructure and staffing training can weigh heavily on institution's budget and so an institution is called to undertake a cost-benefit analysis concerning its investment in digital preservation. The resources available can be used to develop specific services related to the preservation function, which has in any case evaluated with reference to its feasibility in terms of reasonable costs, such as technical training, standards and best practices, consultant services, cooperative or shared storage/access/preservation facility and model policies.

A policy review represents an important cost that depends on frequency with which a digital preservation policy is updated. However, it is widely accepted that, although the costs of preserving digital materials might be high, the cost, consequences and implications of not having a digital preservation policy may be higher and in some cases they could affect the feasibility of the preservation.

MONITORING AND REVIEW

A digital preservation policy should be subjected to reviews to take into account of the technological changes, new standards, etc. moreover, it should be conducted on a routine basis in response to internal or external stimuli or both.

IMPLEMENTATION OF POLICY

An institution that aims at implementing a digital preservation policy needs to assure financial commitment and to adjust active management of digital materials at each stage of their life cycle. Therefore, a programme for digital preservation should be included into the workflow of an organization and should be flexible to adjust itself to new technological developments.

CHALLENGES

The Library plans to "preserve and provide access to the scholarly record." In order to accomplish this plan, it is necessary for the Library's preservation program to face a number of challenges. These challenges include:

- The increasing volume of digital materials to be maintained.
- The rapid evolution of technologies used to capture, store, and represent digital materials.
- Continuing to update staff expertise as technologies change.

- The need to maintain and describe the complex relationships between the components of digital objects.
- Uncertainty about the significant properties or essential characteristics that must be described and maintained for digital resources.
- Intellectual property and other rights-based constraints on providing access.
- The financial commitment necessary to ensure long-term viability of a preservation program.
- Administrative complexities in ensuring cost-effective and timely action to implement preservation strategies.

PRINCIPLES

Digital Preservation will operate in accordance with the following principles:

- Commit to provide continued access to digital materials selected for preservation.
- Commit to taking on the challenges and responsibilities of preserving our own digital materials rather than outsourcing this key function to an outside service provider
- Take action even if no perfect solution exists, but strive to follow current best practices in a new and rapidly evolving field.
- Commit to lifecycle management which includes making decisions of retention, use, and preservation of digital material at the acquisition and/or creation stage.
- Work with producers of digital material to influence the standards and practices they use and to increase their awareness of preservation needs.
- Provide appropriate skills training (digital capture techniques and metadata creation) and increase awareness of digital preservation in the Libraries.
- Keep abreast of technological change and monitor new developments in the digital preservation field, including an awareness of international standards.

- Establish procedures to meet archival requirements pertaining to provenance, chain of custody, authenticity, and integrity.
- Document and identify any remedial treatment, alterations and/or additions to an original object and make them as minimal and reversible as possible.
- Comply with intellectual property, copyright, and ownership rights for all content.
- Clearly and consistently document policies, procedures, and practices and review them on a regular basis.
- Strive to comply with the Open Archival Information System (OAIS) Reference Model standard and the requirements for a trusted digital repository.
- Adhere to prevailing community standards for preserving access to digital content whenever possible.
- Commit to an interoperable, scalable digital archive with appropriate storage management capabilities.
- Consider developing and implementing any and/or all of the following digital preservation strategies as appropriate:
  (a) Technology conservation: maintaining obsolete hardware and software as a means of access in the short to medium term
  (b) Refreshing: copying information content from one storage media to the same storage media
  (c) Migration: transferring digital resources from one hardware/software generation to another.
  (d) Persistent identifiers: the name for a resource that will remain the same regardless of the resource's location, so that links to the resource will continue to work, even if it is moved.
- Select the most appropriate and cost-effective strategy for the preservation of the digital object.
- Identify and describe digital materials using appropriate metadata for resource discovery, management and preservation.
- Use standardized metadata schema as they become

available for interoperability between programs.

- Preserve metadata and always maintain the links between digital objects and their metadata.
- Work collaboratively whenever it is the most appropriate and cost-effective solution.

COLLABORATION

The Libraries recognize that ensuring the long-term preservation of digital materials is a complex and potentially costly endeavor. It may prove too expensive for every cultural heritage institution to build its own technological infrastructure for digital preservation. In addition, we have a commitment to preserving not only our own unique digital content, but also to participating in efforts to preserve the digital scholarly record. For these reasons, the Libraries will seek to work collaboratively on digital preservation efforts where appropriate.

In pursuing collaborative relationships, the Libraries will:

- Identify appropriate partners.
- Establish written agreements on roles and responsibilities.
- Help develop the policies, procedures, and tools necessary to support any collaborative Digital preservation efforts
- Work with the producers of digital content to encourage practices that enable preservation
- Share information on its own experiences, and learn from the experience of others

All collaborative digital preservation activities must be in keeping with the Libraries' own digital preservation policy.

SELECTION AND ACQUISITION

The Library's Collection Development Policy and more specifically, the document Collecting, Digitizing and Storing Digital Content Criteria defines the priorities and criteria for acquiring digital content for long-term digital preservation.

ACCESS AND USE CRITERIA

It is the Libraries' goal to make information available to the widest possible audience. With this goal in mind, digital materials designated by the Collecting, Digitizing and Storing Digital Content Criteria and preserved by the libraries will be made available for access into the future. Each individual digital collection will have its own defined restrictions for access and use. These restrictions may be determined by intellectual property rights, legal requirements, privacy concerns, or mission.

FINANCIAL SUSTAINABILITY

The following areas have identified specific resources to support and enhance its digital preservation function.

(a) Institutional Commitment

To sustain its digital preservation function has allocated a portion of its membership support to digital preservation services. In addition, it continually seeks external research funding to extend its digital preservation scope and capabilities and has secured contracts to fund specific initiatives.

(b) Cooperation and Collaboration

The active and collaborative research program integrates digital preservation requirements and competencies into its priorities and acknowledges digital preservation as a shared community responsibility. The digital policy has long-standing and emerging partnerships with other data archives, other digital repositories, data producers, and data providers in the United States and internationally for digital preservation cooperation and collaboration.

(c) Technological and Procedural Suitability

The majority of digital content in the collections currently consists of social science research data, requisite documentation to use and understand the data, and associated files. Upon receipt of a deposit, the digital content to ensure that confidential information has not been included in the data corrects errors can be filled with gaps in the documentation. and produces distribution versions of the data. Technicians digitize documentation that is received only in hard copy format. The archives of the original digital content has been received the normalized versions of processed data, superseded versions of data that have been distributed. The archived files will enable to retain the ability to regenerate distribution formats over time. For files submitted on physical storage media, the archival being made a archival copies but does not preserve the original transmission media. In terms of documentation,

The digital policy has adopted normalization and migration as its primary digital preservation strategies. Normalization produces file formats for data and documentation that are as close as possible to ASCII for text, or TIFF for images, to enable preservation, and reduces the range of file formats to be preserved to ensure that the digital preservation load is manageable. Migration converts digital content to current file formats as software and related technology evolve and copies digital content from older to newer storage media as part of a systematic program. The digital policy is being investigated appropriate preservation strategies for the expanding range of digital content types in its collections.

(d) System Security

The processing procedures for digital content actively address the need for ensuring the accuracy and completeness of digital content through the careful comparison of documentation and data submitted and the generation of metadata and documentation for data. The implementation of an automated deposit form addressed the need for ensuring the authenticity of digital assets by requesting detailed information and signatures for submission. The digital policy ensures the authenticity and integrity of its digital content through the active and ongoing use of checksums from receipt of the digital content onwards.

The library has developed several lower-level policy and procedural documents that address specific aspects of the long-term protection of its digital assets. For example, Secure Package Handling Procedures are being stipulated the procedure for receiving and sending physical packages containing sensitive data. Procedures for processing requests for restricted data stipulate the steps for responding to requests for restricted data. and policy on receiving data with direct identifiers defines appropriate actions when data received contains a set of principles for protecting digital assets within the context of disaster planning.

(e) Procedural Accountability

As a member organization with a service orientation and as a proponent of good digital preservation practice the concerned library is committed to transparency in its policies and operations and has established a program to develop, promulgate, and maintain a comprehensive set of policies, procedures, and protocols.

(f) Audit and Transparency

The digital library is continued to an ongoing self-assessment and improvement process that aligns policies and practice with the Trustworthy Repositories Audit and Certification (TRAC) requirements that were revised and incorporated into the ISO standards. The concerned library has participated as a test audit in the certification conducted. The library of concerned is committed to a two-year cycle of self-assessment and a five-year audit cycle to evaluate, measure, and adjust the policies, procedures, preservation approaches, and practices of the digital preservation function.

(g) Aspirational Digital Preservation Policies

For organisations not yet doing digital preservation an aspirational policy can be a very useful tool as a proposed commitment to preserving digital records. It does have limitations however when an organisation wants to begin doing digital preservation. When an organisation begins to actively collect and preserve digital records the policy will need to be updated including explicit roles, responsibilities and actions. This will then inform the development of the strategy. Ideally both the policy and a strategy should be in place prior to beginning digital preservation.

(h) Audience of a Digital Preservation Policy

A digital preservation policy must reflect and represent all parties involved in digital preservation why they are involved and their respective responsibilities. It should be written with the intention of informing everyone who may have involvement with digital preservation (directly or indirectly) what is being done and why?

Given the potential wider audience of a policy care should be taken to avoid overly technical language as the wording must comprehensible to anyone engaging with the digital preservation activities. Visibility of the policy is important and it is recommended that a finalised policy be published in an accessible format online for public users and either on an intranet or central location for users within the organization.

RELATIONSHIP WITH DIGITAL PRESERVATION STRATEGY

A digital preservation strategy is the broad approach adopted by an organisation to ensure that the content of digital records remains in a usable form over time. The strategy works by identifying specific triggers which will determine when digital preservation activities may take place. For example:

(a) **Migration** : File formats close to obsolescence are migrated to a more sustainable format

(b) **Ingest** : When records are taken in their file formats under goes a defined normalization process to present the record content in a more sustainable format. Both the policy and the strategy are essential to ensure there is a verifiable and trusted means of preserving the integrity of digital records. Depending on the scale and complexity of digital preservation small organisations may include parts of a strategy within the policy. If this is the case care is needed to ensure changes to the strategy will not require a revision of the policy.

The digital preservation policy must identify a digital preservation strategy and its owner(s). This reinforces the strategy and the preservation activities it defines, whilst allowing the policy to remain independent and not have to be updated when a change is made. The following table 5 shows the different focus of both a policy and a strategy in relation to delivering digital preservation. These are examples and not a full itinerary of what either a policy or strategy may include.

Table 5

Function	Policy	Strategy
Ownership for digital preservation	X	
Strategic Alignment of digital preservation	X	
Coverage of digital preservation	X	
Roles and Responsibilities	X	
Relationship to other policies	X	
Relationship to other documentation	X	
Type of storage for digital records		X
Accepted / Preferred formats		X
Triggers for migration		X
Types of migration		X
Triggers for normalisation		X
Types of normalisation		X

RELATIONSHIPS WITH OTHER DOCUMENTATION

The policy will be underpinned by supporting documentation some of which may already exist that defines how certain processes and business relationships will be managed.

The following table 6 provides examples of supporting documentation and their relationship to the digital preservation policy.

Table 6

Documentation	Relationship
List of accepted / preferred file formats	This is a list of the software file formats (e.g. pdf-A, .doc etc) that the archive will accept. This should not be a fixed list but reviewed periodically and updated to reflect technological changes and the organisation's requirements for preserving new file formats
National / International Standards	The policy should identify any relevant national or international standards which the strategy will work to as means of providing an authoritative approach to

	preservation activities
Legislation	Depending on the content of the records and the organisation(s) they derive from the policy may need to identify specific legislation that defines how and when the records may be accessed / re-used, e.g. Data Protection Act 1998, Copyright, Designs and Patents Act 1988.
Standard Operating Procedures (SOPs)	SOPs should provide instructions on procedures for undertaking digital preservation tasks in a standard way to protect the integrity of the digital records.These SOPs establish a benchmark for performance that current performance can be measured against
Service Level Agreements (SLAs)	SLAs for digital preservation should designate the level and extent of support provided to manage part or all a process within the digital preservation strategy (e.g. Support from an ICT provider to manage the servers used to store the digital records).
Systems Development	Development of new systems or software may result in new types of digital records being produced. The digital preservation policy should provide a mandate for early involvement by those responsible for digital preservation.The earlier an archive can assess digital records (e.g. at creation) the better they will be able to prepare and understand how the digital records should best be preserved.
Formal Contracts	The existence of formal contracts where appropriate reinforces the accountability of service providers and can be referenced by the digital preservation policy as evidence of agreed partnerships

RELATIONSHIP TO OTHER POLICIES

The digital preservation policy will also need to identify what other policies must be taken into consideration when implementing and carrying out digital preservation activities.

The nature of these relationships will need to be articulated indicating where other policies must take precedence.

This table lists the key policies that the organisation may already have established which will have an impact on digital preservation, and consequently must be referenced by the digital preservation policy.

Table 7

Policy	Relationship
List of accepted / preferred file formats	This is a list of the software file formats (e.g. pdf-A, .doc etc) that the archive will accept digital records in. This will not be a fixed list as it should be reviewed periodically and updated to reflect technological changes and the organisation's requirements.
Acquisition / collection policy	An archive must still decide if digital records are of archival value and fall within its collecting remit. These decisions should be determined by the acquisition / collection policy to ensure that the records are of interest to the archive and its users
Analogue Preservation policy	Highlighting a commitment to providing proper preservation for analogue records reinforces the need for preservation across the whole archival collection irrespective of format
Records Management policy	A records management policy clarifies the means by which the organisation manages the aggregation and disposition of its own digital records.These principles are all relevant and may be used to manage digital records that are stored in organised aggregations
Digital Continuity and Information Assurance Policies	A digital continuity policy defines how information should be managed to ensure it remains usable, complete and available to the organisation.It is sensible to use the same processes for archived digital records to give consistent management of all IT systems owned by an organisation.

Freedom of Information /Data Protection policies	Both the Freedom of Information Act 2000 and the Data Protection Act 1998 may have an impact on how digital preservation is managed / delivered.The digital preservation policy must identify the organisations policies for dealing with both pieces of legislation as the authority on responding to information requests
Information security policy	In order to protect the organisation's information assets there will be specific requirements laid out in an information security policy.These rules must be reflected in the digital preservation policy to guard against breaches in the organisation's information security
Copyright Policy	At present the Copyright Law there is no legal right to create copies of records except for certain restricted purposes4. This will need to be taken into consideration for records where the archive is not the copyright owner
Standard Operating Procedures (SOP)	SOPs should provide instructions on procedures for undertaking digital preservation tasks in a standard way to protect the integrity of the digital records.These SOPs establish a benchmark for performance that can then be measured against current performance.
Service Level Agreements (SLAs)	SLAs for digital preservation should designate the level and extent of support provided to manage part or all of the processes within the digital preservation strategy (e.g. Support from an ICT provider to manage the servers used to store the digital records).
Systems Development	Development of new systems or software may result in new types of digital records being produced. The digital preservation policy should provide a mandate for early involvement by those responsible for digital preservation.The earlier an archive can assess digital records (i.e. at creation) the

	better they will be able to prepare and understand how the digital records should best be preserved.
Formal Contracts	The existence of formal contracts, where appropriate, reinforces the accountability of service providers and can be referenced by the digital preservation policy as evidence of agreed partnerships.This agreement should provide specific remedies for breach of agreed service levels.

DIFFERENTIATING ACTIVE AND PASSIVE PRESERVATION

The policy should also identify the extent to which it will use active or passive preservation in the ongoing support of digital preservation. Active preservation is any proactive action taken in the preservation of digital records (e.g. migration of records from at risk formats to a more stable format).

Passive preservation is any action that supports digital preservation but does not engage with the digital records directly (e.g. management and backing up of servers storing digital records). An organisation should already have a Digital Continuity and Information Assurance policy that would support such passive preservation to an extent.

KEY SUCCESS CRITERIA FOR A DIGITAL PRESERVATION POLICY

The policy should be benchmarked against agreed success criteria to ensure that it is created with a clear means of measuring its effectiveness.

Irrespective of the success criteria used they must be realistic and achievable. If the criteria cannot be met there is a significant risk that the subsequent strategy for preserving digital records will be inadequate. This in turn will undermine the confidence that the records being preserved are still authentic.

EXAMPLE SUCCESS MEASURES

The following list provides the key criteria that should be included within a policy: Articulate why digital preservation is important and the risks if it is not done. Identify a responsible senior management role to own and champion digital preservation. Identify who is responsible for the management and support of digital preservation – including required expertise. Provide a clear explanation of the agreed relationships between the archive and other business areas needed to support digital preservation. Identify the digital preservation strategy as the authority on preferred approach to digital preservation activities and what triggers drive them, Be accessible in language and publicly available.

This is not an exhaustive list and depending on the scope and anticipated scale of the work the policy may need to incorporate additional criteria for success.

CONCLUSION

Today, when more and more content and data are born digital or converted to digital to enhance access, archives and libraries, researchers, and institutions grapple with providing effective digital preservation to keep this content accessible not just now but well into the future. In 2012, the academic library with institutional repository, information technology, and special collections and archives, embarked on a year-long process to develop a digital preservation policy framework. The purpose of the framework is to formalize our "…continuing commitment to the long-term stewardship, preservation of, and sustainable access to the library's diverse and extensive range of digital assets."

REFERENCES

1. Cornell University Library, Report of the Digital Preservation Policy Working Group on Establishing a Central Depository for Preserving Digital Image Collections, 2001. *http://www.library.cornell.edu/preservation/IMLS/image_deposit_guidelines.pdf*
2. FCLA Digital Archive (FDA) Policy Guide, 2004. *http://www.fcla.edu/digitalArchive/pdfs/DigitalArchivePolicyGuide1_1.pdf*
3. Harvard University Digital Repository Service Policy Guide, 2007. *http://hul.harvard.edu/ois/systems/drs/policyGuide/DRS_Policy_Guide-Printable.pdf*
4. Illinois Digital Environment for Access to Learning and Scholarship (IDEALS) Digital Preservation Policy, 2009. *https://www.ideals.illinois.edu/bitstream/handle/2142/2383/*

IDEALS_PreservationPolicy_Nov2009.pdf? sequence=4

5. North Carolina Department of Cultural Resources Digital Preservation Policy Framework, 2005. *http://statelibrary.ncdcr.gov/digidocs/publications/policy_framework.pdf*
6. University of Massachusetts Amherst Libraries. Collection Development Policy, 2010. *http://intranet.library.umass.edu/intranet/policies/view_one.cfm?MenuID=21&ID=36*
7. University of Massachusetts Amherst Libraries. Collecting, Digitizing and Storing Digital Content Criteria, 2010. *http://www.library.umass.edu/about-the-libraries/library-policies-and-procedures/criteria-forevaluating-digital-proposals/*
8. University of Massachusetts Amherst Libraries. Guidelines for Digitization, 2011. *http://www.library.umass.edu/assets/aboutus/attachments/UMass-Amherst-Libraries-Best-*
9. PracticeGuidelines-for-Digitization-20110523-templated.pdf
10. University of Massachusetts Amherst Libraries. Three Year Plan 2009-2011. *http://intranet.library.umass.edu/intranet/bulletin board/view_items.cfm?MenuID=5016&CategoryID=4*

5

Electronic Library: Librarian in Changing Activities

Harish Kumar Sahu*

ABSTRACT

This paper attempts the concept of electronic library is information stored electronically and made accessible to users through electronic systems and networks. One of the central tenets of the electronic library is the delivery of information, whenever required, to the user's desktop, wherever that may be. Library professionals therefore, will increasingly need to provide their services in some electronic form rather than accept face-to-face contact with their users. As academics become more willing and more accustomed to using electronic information on a regular basis, they will become increasingly dependent on technology for information access. An additional factor is that in networked environments, information providers can supply their information directly to the end-user and so bypass the library entirely. Thus the move to an electronic information environment will radically alter the way in which a library operates and interacts with its users, and library professionals will need to consider their own future role as intermediaries. It will form a crucial part of an

* Assistant Professor, Pt. Ravishankar Shukla University, Raipur (C.G.)

institution's information service provision and is likely to have a much wider remit than that of the traditional library. Electronic libraries will need to provide a range of new value added services for internally generated and externally acquired academic and scholarly information, and may be involved in the delivery of administrative information as well. However, the primary aim of the electronic library will be to support the institution's learning, teaching, and research, which might change significantly with number of users.

Keywords: Electronic Library, e-library, digital library

INTRODUCTION

The concept of library is going through a revolutionary phase due to the proliferation of electronic resources. Lot of discussions and writings have been made regarding library and electronic media to get a conclusion about what to do in the twenty-first century of computerised era. It is supposed that the libraries are at stake with the challenges of electronic resources. We must first decide whether library and electronic resources, electronic appliances are competitors or not.

It is to be clarified that neither electronic appliances nor the libraries are competitor to each other. Library, which is called now-a-days information centres, cannot be the competitor and in this sense computerisation is by no means greater than the library. More specifically, it should be noted that the computerised system is not at all the information centre and it does not govern a library. On the contrary, it is a machine, acting as preserver, and service provider. It is very much helpful to render the service of a librarian to the user quickly and authentically. The questions of users will get prompt answers at a minimum cost within minimum time. Computer will help to perform duties more accurately and exhaustively according to revered Dr. S.R. Ranganathan. So despite the new challenges of electronic media, information centre or library and the computers will be made for each other. Rather the scope for more accurate and comprehensive information may be extended to the users because of the super capacity of the computers. Electronic media is a prosperous system which will help to give the service quicker, authentic and trace of other related subjects may also be obtained from this. There is no doubt that the usefulness of different electronic areas highlights the sources of information.

CHANGING SYSTEM

There is certainly a transition period where manual system of library is switching over to the modern system. We are being acquainted with the terms e.g. Website, E-mail, Internet, Intranet, TQM etc. In other words, these modern equipments and methods are more challenging, helping and modernising to extend the facilities of the institution to the information seekers which must be our motto. To fulfil this motto, we must have to prepare ourselves to devote our best possible effort to the users and for this we must enrich ourselves through proper training so that we may 'save the time of the reader'. This proper training can enrich a librarian and an information scientist to deliver all available information in a systematic way to the users.

Moreover, their responsibility will increase as the information will be available easily and these can be published in book form easily and in a sense information centres will be good publishers also, which may publish rare books containing rare documents. That is possible only because the computer itself can provide list of different types of information on different aspects and different types of various charts which are definitely of extreme importance for researchers, businessmen, students etc. There are various types of subject areas for discussions under overall preview of LIS. But now a vital and relevant thinking about library and information profession at crossroads is being treated as urgent duty. However, this topic need be resulted after a spontaneous broad careful consultation to abolish the ambiguity regarding the topic to avoid lacunas, flaws and shortcomings in all respects of the application of computer science in library science field.

LIBRARY SERVICES

There is no doubt the any kind of library is to provide all kinds of essential services to the user according to their requirements. As computerisation in LIS is a new thing, a strong well planned infrastructure is needed to modernise the whole system gradually. The infrastructure of the Indian libraries are based on the traditional system, the configuration to be adopted depends on the users library size, service and the number of the users.

In this modern era integrated multi-user library management system is the best contribution of information technology. These systems are no doubt powerful and not very tough to operate so that the library staff can use without knowledge of programming or computer skills. These systems almost minimise the activities of library staffs in acquisition (including initiation of titles, checking of duplication), approval method, placing of order, invoice, accession requisition of payment etc, cataloguing (including thesaurus construction, facility of printed catalogue card, current awareness services e.g. bibliographies, list of recent documents etc.), an automated and simplified but flexible circulation system (including query and report facility on both users collection and circulation transaction). Above all online catalogue, online searches on author, title, subject and facility to prepare documentation list, bibliography etc, are also available to great extent from library automation technology.

Though there are very much facilities open up by the application of IT in LIS, the question is whether these facilities will be applicable and fruitful in a developing country like India where most of the villages are not still enlightened with education, do not have proper library facilities at grass root levels. Because, there is tremendous poverty due to low economic standard which is also a vital problem to avail and implement all modern opportunities. On the other hand library has a great social responsibility in developing and enriching the country as an agent to spread education through the use of information technology. This technology will also educate common users to acquire requisite information. General people will get opportunity is having information about all types of knowledge, all types of subjects through internet connection, and through different software packages.

Library is the best place to encourage common people to interact with computer, E-mail, and utility of different packages which will help the consumers to have their necessary information irrespective of village people and town people. We must see that mere storing and retrieving information is not the only purpose of a library; dissemination of these information will play an important role for advancement of education. Library can only provide referral as well as substantive information in the form of bibliographies, and photocopies of the relevant documents. Computer, multimedia, Internet, different forms of information resources will provide all such information in a centralised process which will be easily accessible and exploitable in fact, information technology will accommodate the increased workload, connect the libraries of different places, decentralise the whole library system and integrate both the users and the library professionals. This will make true to the truest sense of the five laws of Dr. S.R. Ranganathan. For achieving highest effect for library network and information retrieval a well-planned framework and infrastructure have to be framed by the librarians, information technologist for library automation according to the need and capacity of the respective library. Besides, in this age of information explosion or knowledge explosion information technology is the boon to solve the problems. For this one has to plan for a series of activities which the information centre requires i.e. to provide basic facilities for consumers for wide access to libraries:

- To frame an integrated library and information management system which can bring powerful automatic resource control to provide library personnel with more time to devote for other specialised tasks.
- To choose library automation software carefully so that it consists of maintenance facility of authority files, auto-cataloguing, website service on cataloguing, auto import-export service from various web-sites, auto keyboards, AACR2 card format (multilingual), Bar codes, book bank management, intranet system, correspondence kit, E-mail, Internet access etc. for creation of library database on collection of books, serial holdings, bibliography, networking and placement of database on websites.
- To serve this changing society based on information

technology of twentyfirst century, traditional concept of library education obviously require overhauling. A comprehensive professional training programme, emphasis on information technology should be introduced immediately throughout the country which will prepare them to be self-sufficient in handling the new challenging media, equipment and technology and to improve the whole library system. However, the librarian or library manager should also take part in development programme for the illiterate, underdeveloped people of this developing country like India which is overpopulated (more than one hundred crores), where poor people are constrained to sale their child in lieu of money till today, where woman can be burnt or declared as witch by the fellow people. Here the libraries especially local libraries have great role to do something for the advancement of society and to eradicate illiteracy, to overcome all these superstitions, barriers, unhealthy atmosphere.

USE OF INFORMATION TECHNOLOGIES IN ELECTRONIC LIBRARY

The following technologies are relevant to electronic library:

- Computer technologies such as database organisation and management, library management operation.
- Telecommunication technologies such as library networks,information networks, Internet.
- Reprographic technologies includes photography, microfilms, optical/digital, and audio/video materials.
- Library technology which includes traditional functions i.e. classification, cataloguing, data base creation, CAS, SDI, etc.
- Technical communication which involves technical writing, editing and publishing.

CHANGE IN LIBRARY ACTIVITIES

The following activities are involved in the library, which are undergoing the changes:

Collection Development : The information explosion and constant library budget have forced the librarians to change their focus to the development of the information available in database and on online systems. Most of the libraries have been developing collections not only on traditional media (print on paper) but also electronic publications, CD-ROMs and multimedia products. Some of the information is now available in electronic forms such as in the health science there are many publications, which are available on CD-ROM only. Acquisition through Internet is also possible. Linking of new database and e-journals to the library is a new task that nobody properly did.

Cataloguing & classification : The card catalogue is being replaced by online public access catalogue (OPAC) which is a database of holdings of the library.

Circulation : In traditional library this function have great importance but it will reduce their importance as the library switching towards electronic library. Many libraries have their computerised circulation system. Due to the impact of electronics, borrowing of library collections has been reduced to some extent. Moreover, many journals and other documents are available on Internet.

Reference service : Reference librarian has to consult OPAC of his/her library and reference sources, as well as external sources through Internet and other networks for providing reference service. Reference service can be enhanced by e-mail through LAN and WAN. Reader services are given today not only personally but also electronic means.

Preservation & Archiving : Since library acquisition are increasingly in nonpaper forms like CD-ROM, multimedia publication, the preservation measures cover these media also.

Staffing & Training : The new task can not be equally divided according to the old scheme and the additional workload for developing & maintaining the electronic library does not always fit into the existing order. Some tasks are related to the traditional library and some are new. In general, the electronic library is adding many additional duties on the present team. Administratively many libraries are still organised according to old system, which is based on traditional departments i.e.

acquisition, cataloguing, serial control, etc. Duties and hierarchy are usually well defined in this system. It is difficult to change the old hierarchy & duties and it is also not desirable. There is a strong justification for the traditional library organisation, but a flexible and dynamic solution is needed for the areas that are affected by the constant change. Libraries do not yet have enough experience to define all new tasks related to electronic library. Only a different approach will enable the library to cope with the new duties without dramatically changing the administrative manpower organisation of the library. The solution should not be a part of the old hierarchy. The library can create a parallel scheme in which librarians should be treated on an individual basis rather than according to their place and duties in the traditional hierarchy. Special tasks can be given as personal assignments to people with qualifications, ability and enthusiasm to do more and to take part in the new and advanced developments.

The prerequisite to such an approach is an appropriate organisation surrounding with new values. The creation of the correct culture demands investing efforts in employee's education, learning new techniques and constant updating. Most libraries do not get enough additional manpower to compete with new duties related to the electronic library. Most of the work required for the transition into the electronic library areas is done by the existing team. The computer or the PC with its basic software is an essential tool, and librarians should improve their ability to use it constantly. The combination of experienced librarians well trained in modern technology, with personal responsibility to individual or team missions is the key to success and progress.

User education : Library services will be changing to a great extent due to the impact of electronics on library. Thus, librarians have to prepare written explanations and messages to the users/readers regarding new services and giving group instructions on how to use the electronic library.

CONCLUSION

It is important to feel at this juncture that societal change, technological change, and cultural change is going on. So the change in technology will be in each and every room like the television has taken its place in our daily livelihood. This change will also be in the libraries. We will have to accept it and promote it effectively, efficiently, skillfully to abolish the difference between the rural and urban people in access of information and education. We should unite Public Library movement, Adult Education movement and Eradication of literacy movement develop an enlightened society which will be able to utilise and exploit the modern library systems and its services. The reorganisation of the library in order to adopt new techniques and to incorporate the electronic library is sometimes called re-engineering. However, unlike the original definition of re-engineering, which means that the new system replaces the old one, the traditional library is not abandoned or neglected, but is continuing to develop side by side with the electronic library.

The interlibrary ioan and circulation department already requires less manpower as more material is now available directly to the users via network in the electronic library. When electronic version journals will replace the paper editions considerably, the workload of the serial control department will reduce to a great extent.

The library will still need its professional staff, but they should be prepared to perform additional duties frequently. Higher qualifications and constant updating are essential in the future library. The changes in library management and manpower organisation are highly affected by electronic library and this change will determine the future of the library organisation

REFERENCES

1. Dwivedi, S C. (2005). Digital Library. New Delhi: Shree Publishers & Distributers.
2. Gupta, A K. (2012). Digital Library and Education. New Delhi: Pearl Book.
3. Singh, U N. (2004). Information Technology in Libraries. New Delhi: Shree Publishers & Distributers.33-120.

6

Exploring E-resources in Modern Academic Libraries: A Study

Sunil Kumar Satpathy*

ABSTRACT

Due to the changes in library environment, a new type of library resources in the form of electronic resources (popularly known as e-resources) have entered into the library collections and have become more popular than its print counterparts due to their added advantages over print resources. This paper defines the concept of e-resources. Discusses with various advantages and disadvantages associated with the e-resources. Describes the various types of e-resources are available in modern academic libraries. Analyses various steps involved in procurement of e-resources. Concludes with the remarks that initiatives need to be taken to form or strengthen e-resource consortia, so that maximum libraries can get/procure more e-resources and thereby will be able to meet the information need of their users in a better way.

Keywords : E-Resources, Academic libraries, ICT

* Dy. Librarian, National Institute of Technology, Raipur

INTRODUCTION

The advent and development of Information Communication Technology (ICT) have brought remarkable changes on all walk of life .One can see the effect of ICT on every organization irrespective of type, size and location. Peoples are also inclined towards the ICT day by day .Accordingly ICT have changed the library environment drastically, particularly the collections of library. Due to this changes a new type of library resources in the form of electronic resources (popularly known as e-resources) have entered into the library collections and have become more popular than its print counterparts due to their added advantages over print resources. The new generation users are also more comfortable in using e-resources .Hence in any modern academic libraries,e-resources have become essential resources for study, teaching and research. Libraries are also spending more budgets on e-resources to satisfy the information need of their users. Although the usages of e-resources seem to be simple, the selection, procurement and management of e-resources are a complex process. This paper attempts to provide an overview on the various aspects of e-resources in modern academic libraries.

CONCEPT AND DEFINITION

Generally Electronic resources are the information available in digital or electronic format such as e-books, e-journals, e-theses and dissertations etc. These resources are accessed on an electronic device such as computers, laptop, kindle, mobile phone etc. E-resource is short term for Electronic Resources or electronic information resources.

In the words of Saye "electronic resources are the information resources that are generated through some electronic medium and made available to a wide range of viewers both on-site and off-site via some electronic transferring machine or Internet."[1]The e-resources in libraries may be offline i.e. in the form of CD, DVD etc which are accessed through computers or online which are accessed via Internet from remote locations. In the opinion of Swain and Panda," the electronic resources in its ambit include all kinds of digital collections in the form of databases, journals and books, image collections, examination papers, government and official publications, newspapers, patent resources, technical reports, standards, theses/dissertations."[2]

The e-resources are made available for access either through remote access i.e. accessible through computer networks or through direct access i.e. fixed medias such as CD, DVD, cassettes etc.

ADVANTAGES OF E-RESOURCES

The various advantages of e-resources can be summarized as below.

- No physical storage space required for e-resources
- Maintenance cost towards loss and damage of e-resources is zero
- E-resources provide 24X7 access facilities
- Not dependant on library opening hour
- No need to come to library physical to get the required information
- E-resources facilitates exposures to a large quantity of information
- Provides random access facilities with direct link to related documents
- E-resources can be downloaded, saved directly in the computers and print out of the same can be taken
- Provides multi users access facilities
- Authentic usage report of e-resources can be generated as and when necessary
- Training /user education on use of e-resources are provided by the publishers/vendors free of cost

DISADVANTAGES OF E-RESOURCES

Along with multidimensional advantages of e-resources, there are many disadvantages/limitations associated with the e-resources. Some are as follows.

- Initial investment for infrastructure, hardware, software etc to access e-resources is required

- Cost of e-resources is comparatively high
- It is dependent on electricity and network connection
- Not convenient to use as compared to print resources by many
- Prices of e-resources are not uniform for all academic institutions
- License agreement is to be sing with the publishers which is a legal document having many confusion
- Platform/hosting fee for e-resources are charged by some publishers, which is additional financial burden for the institute
- Removal of contents from purchased/subscribed e-resources by the publishers
- Misuse of information by the users ,violating copy right issues

TYPES OF E-RESOURCES IN LIBRARIES

The e-resources are of various types which may include newspapers to magazines,journals, books, theses and dissertations etc. Further it may be offline or online. The offline e-resources are earlier form of e-resources where information are stored in digital form and are accessed offline by the computer. These e-resources are stored and organized in libraries with the help of Mirror server. Previously the educational study materials, encyclopedias, dictionaries, e-books, e-databases (abstracting and indexing), course materials etc were available in CD/DVD form .But with the development of Internet, more and more e-resources have become online.The major types of e-resources available in modern academic libraries are discussed below.

E-journals : E-journals are the electronic version of a journal ,which may be available offline in the form of CD/DVD or online via Internet .But in practice most of the e-journals now a days are available online, contains full text of the journals, and available mostly on yearly subscription basis.

Depending upon the contents and presentation e-journals may be full text or non-full text journals. The full text journals contain full paper along with abstract, references etc as in case of print journals. Further the full text journals are available in both prints+ online or only online. Example of some full text e-Journals are the journals published by Elsevier, Springer, Sage, Taylor & Francis, NISCAIR, Publishing India group etc.

Similarly the non full text journals does not contains the full text of all papers of the journals and may contains full text of certain papers and abstract of others like Bulletin of Menninger clinic. Also certain non full text journals contains abstract such as Chemical Abstract and sometimes Table of contents(TOC) only. Besides many open access e-journals are now available which are peer reviewed journals and are being published by reputed publishers and many governmental organizations, universities etc.

E-databases : E-Databases are nothing but collections of various types of e-resources mostly on a particular discipline. It may be synonymously termed as "online database". Wikipedia defines an online database as "a database accessible via a network, now generally the Internet. It differs from a local database, held in an individual computer or its attached storage such as CD".[3]

E-database contains different types of e-resources such as e-books, e-journals, conference proceedings, transactions, magazines etc in their respective domain. For example in engineering & technology the databases available are IEL online, Science Direct, ASCE, ASME, ACM etc, in medicine field the databases available are MedIND, MEDLINE ,in agriculture the database available are AGRIS, AGRICOLA, in management the databases are Emerald, EBSCO, ProQuest etc, in social sciences the databases available are SSRN eLibrary, Visindi etc.

E-databases may also be full text databases containing full text of the e-resources(Ex-MedIND in the field of biomedicine, IEL online in the field of engineering etc), bibliographic containing only bibliographic information(Ex-Inspec, the leading bibliographic database in the field of science, engineering and technology; Pubmed, the citation database for biomedical literature, IndMED, the bibliographic database of Indian biomedical literatures), non-full text contains abstract of the e-resources(Chemical Abstract, LISA) contains in the database.

Online Journal Archive (OJA) : OJA are basically the back volumes of journals which are available subject wise and online. It consists the full text of a numbers of journals form its Volume-1, Issue-1 to a particular year. This e-resource has replaced the back volume sections of the libraries and has been proved useful for the researchers in doing literature search for their research.

E-books : In the opinion of Satpathy "E-books are electronic form of books where information are organized in a particular order similar to the print book .Although in the initial stage of e-book development ,CD-ROM version of e-books were available where as now almost all e-books are available Online. E-books form an emerging and rapidly changing scholarly platform and are becoming popular day by day"[4]. These are similar to print books but are in digital form to be accessed through computer via Internet or down able on a hardware device. According to Lee, "an e-book is a term used to describe a text analogous to a book that is in digital form to be displayed on a computer" [5]. The e-books can be read with the help of computers ,tablets, Smart mobile phones, Kendels etc .A large number of e-books are being published now a days by almost all reputed publishers such as Elsevier, Wiley, Springer, McGraw Hill, Oxford University Press, Cengage learning etc in all subjects .The e-books are available either in bundles/packages or individual e-book title basis. These e-books have occupied a remarkable portion of library collection in academic libraries more particularly in University and central Government funded libraries such as IITs and NITs libraries. The e-books can be procured directly for the publishers or through vendor or aggregators. Some e-books are also freely available in the Internet, called as Open Access e-books.

E-Theses and Dissertations (ETD) : Previously it was a herculean task for libraries to store theses and dissertations in the libraries .Also it was a difficult task for researchers to visit various libraries and find the thesis or dissertations on the related areas of their research. With the development of technology, over past few years these resources are being digitized and stored in libraries in electronic form. Various controlling bodies of academic institutions such as U.G.C, AICTE , and MHRD etc have made it mandatory to submit electronic version of thesis/ dissertations along with the print version. The Sodhaganga of UGC, National Digital Library (NDL) project of MHRD are few examples of this. Apart from this, many universities, Central Funded Institutions and Research organization are maintaining their ETD and are making available it to public. This has made easy the storage and maintenance work of libraries. Many proprietary software and open source software such as Green Stone Digital Library (GSDL) software, D-Space, E-print etc available to create and maintain ETD in libraries.

E-**newspapers** : Keeping pace with the changing IT age, now a day almost all national and state level daily newspapers have gone online along with its print version. Accordingly many modern libraries have started to subscribe online news papers which have been appreciated by the users. Some IT firms have also developed news papers kiosks by which libraries can access full text of a large number of news papers of various countries and languages. For example Total IT solutions Pvt. Ltd has developed Library Press Display-the Newspaper Direct, the world's largest online newspaper and magazine kiosk, where one can access more than 1700+ Publications from 95 Countries in 51 Languages .One can also browse his/her favorite newspapers, search or monitor the news for specific articles of interest, listen to a newspaper, share stories with friends through email or your blog or take it on the road, PressDisplay.com brings it altogether in a website.

PROCUREMENT OF E-RESOURCES IN LIBRARIES

The e-resource procurement in libraries is a complex task and involves a number of steps. It also needs to be done carefully since these are not physically available in libraries and large amount of library budget are spent on this.

Invitation of requisition from the departments and users: The initial step for any library is to invite recommendations from various departments and also research scholars and students. Then these e-resources are listed and scrutinized according to the target users, price of e-resources, library budget, terms and conditions of supply etc.

Locate the e-resources : The next step is to locate the e-resources means to find out its publishers .Then it is decided that whether a particular e-resources are to be procured directlyfrom publishers or through any aggregator/vendor. If a particular e-resource is subscribed for the first time, then library may go for a trial access which most of the reputed publishers provide for 15 to 60 days. On the basis of usage reports of trial access and user's response, final decision may be taken.

Placing order : The next step is to placing order for the e-resources to the publishers/aggregators/vendors. But before placing order, it is very much important to negotiate price of the e-resources and terms and conditions of supply with the suppliers. If the price of e-resource is negotiated by consortia, then there is no need of further price negotiation.

The e-resources can be procured:

(a) Directly through the publisher like Elsevier, Emerald etc

(b) Through the vendors like GIST, Gurgaon, Allied publisher subscription agency

(c) Through aggregator like Ebsco, Informatics (India) Limited.

(d) Through some organization/association which publish open access journals like NISCAIR, DESIDOC.

(e) The order for e-resources may be done on yearly subscription mode (mostly for e-journals, e-database) or onetime payment mode (mostly for e-books, OJA etc)

Promotion of e-resources : After procurement of e-resources, the next important step is to promote the use of e-resources by the libraries. Libraries have to take a proactive role in informing the availability of e-resources in libraries to their users through notices, various social networking sites, institutewebsites, information brochures etc. The basic role of libraries are to ensure the accessibility of procured e-resources. To popularize and maximize the use of e-resources, various users education program, training programs need to be organized by the libraries inassociations with the publishers. Also regular usage report are to be generated, evaluated and necessary steps may be taken by the libraries and institutes for its proper use. The usage reports are also important for taking decision for renewal of e-resources.

CONCLUSION

E-resources have become an integral and essential part of library collections.The quality of library collections and services are measured largely on the basis of types and quantity of e-resources available in the libraries.At the same time with the shrinking library budget, it has become a difficult task for library managers, particularlyof small or privately managed academic libraries to accommodate the e-resources as per the demand of the users. The infrastructure facilities available-resource in most of the libraries or academic institutions is not encouraging. Hence initiatives need to be taken to form or strengthen e-resource consortia, so that maximum libraries can get/procure more e-resources and thereby will be able to meet the information need of their users in a better way.

REFERENCES

1. Saye,J.D.(2001). The organization of electronic resources in the library and information science curriculum. OCLC systems and services,2,71-78
2. Swain,D.K & Panda,K.C(2011). Use of e-resources in libraries of Management Institutions. New Delhi: SSDN Publishers and Distributors.
3. Wikipedia, ***http://en.wikipedia.org/wiki/***
4. Satpathy,S.K.(2013). Challenges and opportunities of Electronic Librarianship: Experience of Academic libraries.In R. K. Mahapatra (Ed). Electronic Librarianship: issues & trends (pp.63-72). New Delhi:SSDN Publishers & Distributors.
5. Lee, L.A & Wu, M.M. (2002). Do librarians dream of of electronic materials? A beginners' guide to formal selection. The Bottone: Managing library Finances. 3, 102-109.

7

Negotiating Issues Related to License Agreements for Electronic Resources in Digital Environment: An Analytical Study

Prof. Subarna Kr. Das*

ABSTRACT

License Agreements are very vital issues for electronic documents. Licensors use license agreements to grant their licensees the right to use certain intellectual property, including software, trademarks, service marks, inventions, and patents. Besides the property being licensed and the royalty rates, license agreements can also include representations, warranties, termination provisions, terms of indemnification and dispute resolution clauses. Agreements include a scope of issues such as exclusivity or territorial restrictions, financial aspects, royalty rates, and so forth. Present paper attempt to highlights the various issues related to License Agreement for electronic resources in the changing context of digital environment.

* Professor and Former Head, Jadavpur University, Kolkata

Keywords : Library and Information Centres, Electronic Information, Intellectual Property Rights, Licensing Agreement, Electronic Information Sources,

INTRODUCTION

As information sources are shifted from the print to the electronic form, the outright sale of information sources are becoming less common and the leasing of information source is becoming more popular in the recent years. Generally, libraries must purchase electronic information source-databases by license agreements with the publishers of this information sources. The library community's response to these developments has been the creation of principles for the licensing of electronic resources and the drafting of standard license agreements to be used with electronic materials. However, most license agreements currently in use are prepared by publishers and therefore favor their positions. Unfortunately, librarians generally are uncomfortable with negotiating electronic license agreements. Few librarians negotiate contracts on a regular basis and even fewer are trained in the negotiation of contracts. Librarians should be more particular of publisher agreements and scrutinize them carefully to ensure they do not restrict the needs of their users.

LICENSING AGREEMENT

A licensing agreement is a partnership between an intellectual property rights owner (licensor) and another who is authorized to use such rights (licensee) in exchange for an agreed payment (fee or royalty). A variety of such licensing agreements are available, which may be broadly categorized as follows:

- Technology License Agreement
- Trademark Licensing and Franchising Agreement
- Copyright License Agreement
- Every License Agreement should contain a framework - a skeleton - which provides support for other clauses or systems of clauses in the License Agreement. Sometimes these skeletal elements are scattered throughout the Agreement and, due to awkward

Drafting, can be difficult to find. The skeleton of a License Agreement is:

(a) Identification of the Parties
(b) Recitals
(c) Definitions
(d) License Grant
(e) Compensation
(f) Obligations of the Parties
(g) Term and Termination
(h) Conflict Resolution
(i) Other Common Clauses

LICENSE AGREEMENTS & ELECTRONIC INFORMATION SOURCES

One of the major development in libraries and information services in the last 20 years has been the introduction and spread of electronic information sources (EIS). The commonly available EIS, namely, online databases, online journals, the Internet, and other networked information sources, are competing with, and in some instances replacing, the print-based information sources as the primary media for the storage and communication of recorded information content. The demand for e-resources by the academic and research community has increased day by day. The e-resources enable the academic user to access a large number of scholarly journals from reputed publisher, aggregators and societies. With the entrance of these electronic resources into the resource- market, both publishers and librarians felt the importance of license agreement needed for both side for better understanding as well as management of these resources. License agreements require libraries to screen for status before allowing access. Some e-resources require passwords for authentication. The most common strategy for authentication is to register campus IP addresses, the official Internet identification numbers for computers located on each institution's secure network. If you access e-resources from a campus computer, your IP address is recognized and access granted. If you want to access e-resources from home, you may need to do so by going through a university computer with a recognized IP address. You can do this by connecting through the campus modem pool or through the library's "proxy server." In either case, not every electronic journal title will be available full-text due to space limits on the server. Also some publishers of electronic resources do not permit remote access and may limit use of their product to one building or one site. Some e-resources are only accessible via passwords available from the reference desk. Check with the reference desk if you have trouble accessing an e-resource.

APPROPRIATE USE OF LICENSED ELECTRONIC INFORMATION RESOURCES

- limit uses to non-commercial, educational, or personal research purposes
- not facilitate unauthorized access by others (i.e. do not share your network user name and password) .In addition,

You may:	You may not:
Print, download or quote limited amounts of information (with proper attribution)	Systematically download large amounts of information (e.g. download all articles in a journal issue; engage in large-scale downloading from licensed resources to create large databases)
Copy an article for your personal use in teaching or research.	Sell or distribute articles to individuals, institutions, or organizations for commercial purposes.
Create a link to a journal article on a publisher web site	Post a copy of a published article to a University server

NEGOTIATING POINTS

Following are some issues for negotiating license agreements.

Pricing

With the advent of electronic license agreements, many pricing mechanisms are available to both publishers and libraries. Libraries would generally favour the pricing model which provides them the multi user access facility. In additions to that pick and choose option from a bundle of on line databases would fulfill the requirements. In border sense it includes either flat fee subscription agreements or go for a pay-per-view pricing mechanism or a pay-per-view plus free views of an item after the initial view.

In this context, librarians must carefully consider the pricing mechanism offered by the publisher and make sure the use of materials is clearly understood along with the price consequences. Most of the engineering institutes and universities recently completed a multiyear study on the pricing of electronic serials. One preliminary conclusion from this study is that librarians' expectations about the use of serials do not match the reality of how patrons use serials. Users tend to use a relatively small number of journals in their area of interest, but to use those journals intensively.Librarians should understand how patrons use information resources in order to make better-informed decisions about negotiating prices for electronic access. If users tend to use or select few journals intensively, the purchase of a subset of an aggregate database, rather than the entire database, may be more appropriate.

Users

The definition of the term "users" becomes very important in electronic license agreements. When dealing with the purchase of printed materials, the definitions of "users" was taken for granted because the general law of copyright defined that term. But the license agreement must define "users." Librarians must carefully consider who should fall within the definition of "users" within their particular library community. "Users" should at least include the current faculty, research scholars, and students of that particular institute.

Access

Librarians must consider how users will access the electronic material. Will passwords be necessary for access to the materials or are IP addresses sufficient? Will access be allowed off campus, which is particularly important for scholars and students who wish to work from their homes. The mode of access to the electronic materials is closely related to the nature of users and should be carefully considered prior to entering into an electronic licensing agreement. Because the management of passwords assigned to users can be complicated and time-consuming, access via IP address is preferred over access by password.

Uses

A patron's use of print materials and electronic materials should be equivalent. there should be an explicit statement in the license agreement that fair use principles apply to the digital materials licensed under the agreement to make clear the library and its users have the right to use these materials as they would print materials. Most users reasonably expect that they can use all materials in the library in a similar manner, unless specifically told otherwise. In other words, there should be no restrictions in the electronic license agreement that would be more restrictive than that pro-vided under the copyright law for printed materials.

INDEMNIFICATION/LIMITATION OF LIABILITY

Generally, in a database license, the library customer should not indemnify the publisher for anything. This includes library users violating copyright law in their use of the electronic materials. The library simply does not have control over how users will use the materials. However, the library should agree to make reasonable efforts to correct or address misuse of which it has actual knowledge. The circulation of user guide or patron orientation in this context would be very much effective in this regard. These reasonable efforts may include denying access to a user who has used the electronic material in violation of copyright law. The publisher, on the other hand, should indemnify the library from certain claims, specifically for claims of copyright infringement related to the content of the database. The publisher is selling a product and therefore it should warrant that it has permission to use any copyrighted material in its database. The knowledge of whether it has obtained these permissions is wholly within the control of the publisher; therefore, the publisher, not the library, should bear this risk.

SIGNATORIES

The librarian should determine what is the appropriate legal entity to sign the license agreement. Once the exact entity name is determined, the librarian must determine who has authority to sign a contract. The librarian should retain a copy of the executed contract and should ensure that an archive of all the license agreements for which the library is legally responsible is maintained.

RENEWAL OF LICENSE

Librarians should also be concerned with the term and duration of the license agreement. Generally librarians should be able to renew the license at their option with prior written notice to the publisher. The library should be required to deliver the written notice to the publisher within a reasonable amount of time, such as thirty to forty five days, prior to the termination of the license. The notice of renewal should be delivered to the librarian so that there is sufficient time to evaluate the continued need of the electronic product and ensure the price charged is a reasonable value for the library. However most of the publishers today offering online renewal facility with the electronic transfer of required amount to a particular bank account. But that should be preferred carefully.

EARLY TERMINATIONS

The license agreement should specifically define the reasons for early termination and should give both parties an opportunity to cure any default within a reasonable period. A large organization, either the library or the publisher, may inadvertently cause a technical default; therefore, written notice and a reasonable opportunity to cure any default should be allowed by the terms of the contract.

UPDATES OR UPGRADES TO SOFTWARE

Ideally, the librarian should also ask for any upgrades to the searching software. The difference between an update and an upgrade is a fine distinction and there is not yet a common understanding of the difference in legal meaning between these terms. In common parlance, an upgrade is a change to software to which a customer is not entitled unless the license agreement specifically provides for it. Therefore, the library must be very careful of the needs the license agreement is intended to fulfill and make sure that the library has a right to obtain any changes in the product that the library will need in the future. This need for updates or upgrades becomes more critical as the duration of the license agreement lengthens.

CONCLUSION

Publishers of electronic materials have strategically employed license agreements to sell their products. License agreements provide a continuous revenue stream compared to one-time sales of printed materials. Publishers also have been concentrating the legal position that copyright law does not apply to digital materials in the same way it applies to printed materials with the goal of improving the profitability of electronic information. The library community has responded to these developments by creating principles for the licensing of electronic resources and drafting standard license agreements.

REFERENCES

1. Hughes, Justin.(2003). Fair use across time. *www.uclalawreview.org/* articles/ archives/
2. Jewell, T.D. (2001). Selection and presentation of commercially available electronic resources: issues and practices. *www.arl.org/stats/specproj/jewell.html*
3. Johnson, R.K. and J. Luther (2007). The e-only tipping point for journals: what's ahead in the print-to-electronic transition zone. www.arl.org
4. Muir, Adrienne (2003). Copyright and licensing for digital preservation. *http://www.cilip.org.uk/publications/update magazine/archive/archive2003/june/update0306c.htm*
5. *www.gist* .in (Visited on 12/9/2015)

8

Role of E-resources Sharing in Rural Academic Development

Nidhi Gupta *

ABSTRACT

No library, however big it may be, is able to satisfy all the needs of its clientele due to various constraints. It is because of this phenomenon that the concept of resource sharing has developed. Initially the term used for resource sharing activities was library cooperation. Though cooperation theoretically could embrace almost all library activities, practically it was confined to inter-library loan of library documents. But due to physical distance and other reasons even this limited system of cooperation was not being practiced widely. However, with the advent of ICT and its application in library activities, new opportunities opened up for greater cooperation among libraries. At the global level Internet and at the national and local level several library networks came in vogue and databases created for information sharing. In recent years availability of information resources in digital or electronic medium has further facilitated exchange of information resources among libraries, thus creating favorable condition for increased resource sharing.

* Asst. Professor, Dr. C. V.Raman University Bilaspur (CG)

Indian information professionals, education specialists and scientists have realized that the time has come to share the information resources and to coordinate mechanisms. A large number of library resource sharing networks like the Metropolitan Area Networks such as CALIBNET in Calcutta, DELNET in Delhi, BONET in Bombay, PUNENET in Pune, MALIBNET in Madras, HYLIBNET in Hyderabad, ADNET in Ahmedabad, and countrywide ones like ERNET (Educational and Research Institutions), INFLIBNET (Universities and Research Institutions) and DESINET (Defence Laboratories), and sectoral ones like BTISNET (Biotechnology Networks) etc. are under various stages of conceptualization, design, development and implementation. The present study briefly highlights some of the major library networks in India and need of resource sharing, function of resource sharing, forms of resources sharing, also we shall discuss what the limitation of resource sharing are.

Keywords : E-resources, Electronic Library, Digital Library, E-resources sharing

INTRODUCTION

The fundamental aim of the rural library is to provide timely, pertinent, accurate and reliable information services to all the rural community. The rural library helps different sectors of the community by providing right information to the right reader at the right time. For example, it will help children to create reading habit, unemployed youths to get better jobs and farmers to improve agricultural production. Libraries of all countries are functioning for social development by extending these activities and services, sharing books, extension lectures on various topics such as child labor, epidemic diseases, reading habits and environmental protection.

No library or resource center of the world is self sufficient to meet the various information needs of the users.The rapid growth of publications, knowledge explosion, shrinking resources, escalation of prices and ever increasing expectation of users compelled the library and information centers to go for networking for resource sharing. The most important goal of networking is to maximize the availability of resources and services at minimum expenses. Most of the academic libraries are struggling for continuation of current periodicals and purchase of new books. These academic institutions can cope with this problem only by networking and resource sharing. Networking of library and information centers has been recognized as the de facto standard for better resource mobilization in the libraries. Advancement in computing technologies for standardization of bibliographic resources has contributed the steady growth of bibliographic databases in the LICs. A networked system of libraries bears promises to achieve common benefits i.e. sharing of resources, designing better access routes to remote resources, by adopting the best standard for bibliographic databases. Considerable progress has been made in the areas of library networking in India. Several local, metropolitan, regional and national level library networks have already been established in India for resource sharing. The main purpose of all these networks is to acquire reading materials collectively, avoid duplication, consortia approach for costly foreign journals and databases, maximum utilization of reading materials available in libraries of a particular locality or region by the users.

AIMS AND OBJECTIVES

The basic aims and objectives of library networks are:

- To find out the services offered by the respective academic rural libraries.
- To find out the present status of automation of academic libraries in India.
- To suggest a plan for introducing networking of academic rural libraries.

CONCEPT OF RESOURCE SHARING

Generally, the concept of 'Library Co-operation' emerged for rendering better services to users' community through borrowing & lending of documents in formal manner. 'Library Resources' is the term that applied to personnel, material, functions or activities available in a library for satisfying the human needs & demands to acquire their desired knowledge. Library co-operation is a very old concept and a form of resource sharing. The new object of resource sharing has changed the old concept due to multi-dimensional growth of published documents through R&D activities in recent past, cost of the information, advancement of newly invented technologies for information processing and dissemination, etc. Resource sharing entails apportioning, allocating, distributing or contributing something on a voluntary basis for mutual benefits among a group of libraries with a view to achieving best utilization of resources by the ultimate users at a wider level. For better utilization of resources, participating libraries should come together and co-operate in two broad areas: (a) developing the collection on shared basis; and (b) improving services for exploiting such collection

MODEL OF RURAL LIBRARIES

Manipur suggested one model, if the situation warrants in order to meet all the information requirements of village people and to uplift the socio-economical, political, cultural and

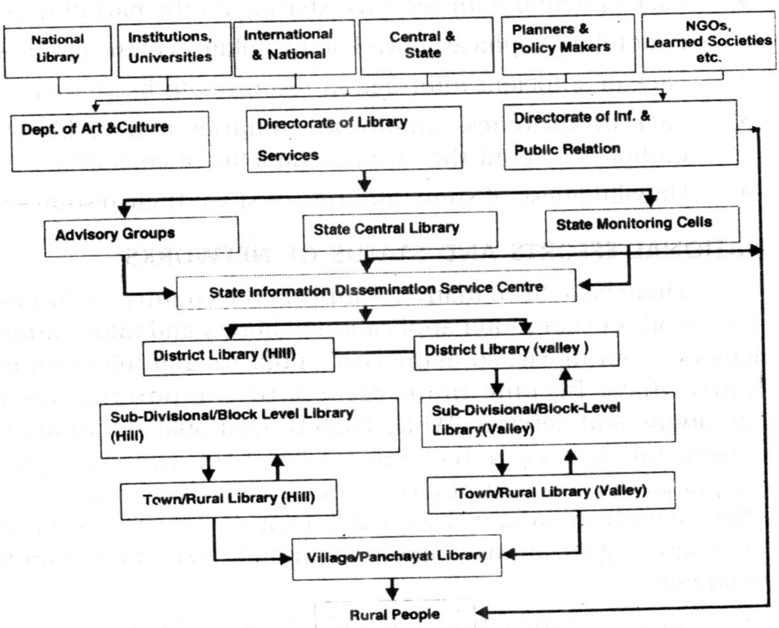

Fig. Model for Rural Library System

all round development of the rural community for the construction of information oriented or knowledge based society in the state of Manipur. The purpose model will facilitate for improving the existing system and services in building up a healthy and progressive rural community. It also help rural people to make use of information resources, acquire, store, assemble, retrieve, and disseminate the right information to the rural people and can access the information at local, regional, national and international level if the system or centre have extended its network facilities abroad. On the basis of the existing infrastructure, and considering the needs and requirement of the rural communities, views and the suggestions of the user communities a model viz. "Rural Library Information Network System" (RLINS).

LIMITATIONS OF E-RESOURCES SHARING

- Uneven development of libraries of different sectors and slow progress of library automation
- Lack of demand for resource sharing on the part of users
- Poor bibliographical control of the holdings of the libraries
- Lack of sufficient information resources to be shared
- Lack of awareness among the libraries and/or library authorities about the ultimate benefits of consortia
- Unwillingness of some libraries to share their resources

NATIONAL EFFORTS AND STATUS OF NETWORKS

There have been many attempts in the country in the last two decades in computer application to library and information activities. During last so many years, libraries and information centres have become more earnest to computerize their operations and services. While NISSAT (National Information System for Science & Technology) has been promoting an integrated approach in library automation in the country, the efforts have been by and large, at the institutional level. Some of the major organizations engaged in computerized information handling are:

- BARC - Bhabha Atomic Research Centre, Mumbai
- DESIDOC - Defence Scientific Information and

Documentation Centre,Delhi

- DRTC - Documentation Research and Training Centre, Bangalore
- IISc - Indian Institute of Science, Bangalore
- IIT - Indian Institute of Technology (Delhi, Chennai Kanpur)
- INSDOC - Indian National Scientific Documentation Centre, New Delhi
- NIC - National Informatics Centre, New Delhi
- NISSAT - National Information System for Science and Technology, New Delhi
- PRL - Physical Research Laboratory, Ahmedabad
- TIFR - Tata Institute of Fundamental Research, Mumbai

Besides the above, University Grants Commission (UGC), Department of Electronics, Department of Telecommunication, Planning Commission and other various Departments of Government of India have also been engaged in establishing various networks. There are possibilities of mounting bibliographical databases on these networks for providing online access-to-access.

The growth of Indian Library Networks may be traced to the efforts made during the last forty years. The chronology is given below:

1958 1958 Scientific Policy Resolution. It was adopted at the instance of Pt. Jawaharlal Nehru. It emphasized the fostering of scientific temper in people. In pursuance of this agenda, several committees and commissions were appointed to look into specific issues and come up with necessary recommendations.

1959 Sinha Committee Report

1965 Ranganathan Report to University Grants Commission (UGC)

1972 V A Kamath Report

1977 Establishment of NICNET by NIC (1975)

1983 Technology Policy Statement. It emphasized the need for a technology information base.

1984 Working group of the Planning Commission headed by Dr N Seshagiri recommended to the govt. the need for modernization of library services and information during Seventh Five Year Plan (1985-90)

1986 NISSAT initiated the establishment of CALIBNET, Calcutta

1988 The National Policy in Library and Information System submitted in 1988. It recommended using of information technology on a national level.

1988 The UGC established INFLIBNET

1992 NISSAT supported the establishment of DELNET, DELHI

1993 NISSAT supported the establishment of ADINET, Ahmedabad.

1993 INSDOC supported the formation of MALIBNET, Chennai.

1994 NISSAT supported the establishment of MYLIBNET, Mysore

1995 NISSAT supported the establishment of BALNET, Bangalore

PRESENT SCENARIO OF LIBRARY NETWORKING IN INDIA

The present status of library networking in India is that most of the libraries covered by some network are creating databases of their holdings and in automating the library activities. Generally, the periodical holdings are attempted first in building up the databases as it takes less time than for the other types of library documents. This is followed by the databases of holdings of books, reports, dissertations, standards, etc. The Library Network Centres, i.e., the coordinating agencies of the networks also are concentrating on acquiring them to provide the user with access to the total records. They provide such access either by email or online through the telephone network. In addition, these centres also try to provide a common software for database development and automation of library activities and services.

Table below gives the details of status of some important library networks in the country;

Name	Year of starting	Promoting Agency	Database development & other activities
ADINET (Ahmedabad)	1993	Society, INFLIBNET & NISSAT	• Library holding database in progress • Library automation in progress • Training programme • Database of current periodicals in member libraries
BALINET (Bangalore)	1995	NISSAT	• Activity will start after getting financial support from NISSAT
BONET (Mumbai)	1994	NCST & NISSAT	• Online union catalogue of periodicals • Online request system for ILL • E-mail and Internet access • Online searching of foreign database • Database on computer • CD-ROM database searching • Database of contents of Indian periodicals • Software for OPAC
CALIBNET (Calcutta)	1992 (1986)	NISSAT	• Library automation in progress • Access to Internet and Dialog • CD-ROM database searching
DELNET (Delhi)	1990 (1988)	Society, NIC & NISSAT	• Books database • Multi-lingual book database • E-mail service • Union list of current periodicals • Database of Indian specialists • Online searching of foreign databases
INFLIB NET	1991 (1988)	UGC	• Union catalogue of 50,000 records • Database of periodicals (30,000 records) • Contents with Abstract Services (COPSAT)

		• Training programme for university library staff
MALIBNET 1993 (Chennai)	Society & INSDOC	• Current serials database • Journal contents database (1,00,000) records • All INSDOC databases on MALIBNET • Automative engineering database (4,500 records) • Access to Internet and Knight Ridder (Dialog) database • CD-ROM database searching
MYLIBNET 1994 (Mysore)	Society, Mysore Library Consortium & NISSAT	• Library automation in progress
PUNENET 1992 (Pune)		

INFORMATION NETWORK ON RURAL DEVELOPMENT

The Center on Integrated Rural Development for Asia and the Pacific (CIRDAP) initiated an Information Network on Rural Development (INRD) in 1992. CIRDAP is an intergovernmental organization of 11 countries, headquartered in Bangladesh. The mandate of the Center is to promote national action in its member countries to develop rural areas and alleviate poverty. One of its objectives is dissemination of information for supporting its programs. It is in pursuance of these objectives that CIRDAP initiated INRD in Bangladesh, with the participation of 24 libraries working in the area of rural development. INRD is a loosely structured network of libraries, with CIRDAP assuming the role of facilitator. The objectives of INRD as identified by the members are to promote the use and exchange of information on rural development and poverty alleviation by sharing resources; to improve the capability of network members to collect, process and disseminate information; to assist network members to use new information technology; and to assist in developing the skills of information personnel. A working committee of seven members has the responsibility to plan and implement network activities. The working committee members are rotated periodically to ensure a participatory decision making process, rather than a centralized one. The working committee meets every quarter to review past activities and plan for the next quarter. In the first year the activities consisted of the following:

- Exchanging information on literature generated by the parent organizations, with special emphasis on non–conventional literature;
- Preparing a periodicals holdings list of the network members;
- Disseminating information on organizational activities such as seminars, workshops, and ongoing research;
- Upgrading professional skills through training; and,
- Providing inter–library lending and reference facilities.

INRD has been in operation for a little over a year. During this period three issues of a bulletin containing the publications of network members have been published. A format for reporting data has been prepared following the format recommended by the Library Association of Bangladesh. The data, entered into the CIRDAP bibliographic database using CDS/ISIS, are made available on diskette or as hard copies to users. Eleven libraries have regularly provided inputs to the database.

POINTS OF CONSIDERATION

One year is too short a time to make an evaluation of INRD activities, but some of the more important issues regarding its organization, activities, and finances are highlighted in the following paragraphs.

Organization

For the present, CIRDAP functions as the coordinator of INRD activities. The experience of many networks is that the focal point becomes the core of its structure, bearing the main responsibility for sustaining network activities. The membership assumes the role of passive observers or receivers of services in return for bibliographic data inputs. The formation of a working committee, with the provision for the periodic rotation of its members, is expected to make the INRD decision-making process participatory, involve members in the design and development of the substantive work of the network, and ensure a collective approach to networking. This approach is also expected to facilitate the withdrawal of CIRDAP as INRD coordinator.

Membership

INRD membership comprises libraries working in the area of rural development and poverty alleviation. They range from government departments and ministries to international organizations to local and foreign non-government organizations. In some of these organizations information is perceived as important, while in others it is on the periphery of organizational activities. Staffing patterns vary from the professional to the non-professional.

Activities

The program of work for the first year included activities that would immediately benefit members and their users. Providing access to the library collections of network members was one activity that could be carried out without much difficulty. All libraries have agreed to provide access to their collections, and make photocopying facilities available at nominal charges.

Many of the organizations to which the network participants belong are engaged in research project implementation. Local, regional and international initiatives and efforts are taken, which produce information ranging from basic facts, to plans which are documented as feasibility studies, project reports, research studies, evaluation reports, etc. Most of this literature is unpublished and remains confined within the agency concerned with such activities. Network members, realizing the need for access to such documentation, agreed to share documents generated by their organizations. CIRDAP collates the information for dissemination through a regular bulletin. In the absence of a national system to collect such information, the INRD effort at disseminating it to the development community is a significant step towards gaining bibliographic control of national non–conventional literature.

Most of the network participants have followed training programs conducted by CIRDAP in using the CDS/ISIS software program for information storage and retrieval. This training supports the development of a computer based information network. CIRDAP attempted to develop a standard format for information exchange, keeping in view the format recommended by the Library Association of Bangladesh. Since most of the libraries are in the early stages of computerization, the adoption of a uniform data entry format becomes feasible. Computerization will also facilitate the integration of the databases of the network members, doing away with the necessity of preparing bulletins to disseminate information; and computerization will reduce the need for additional staff. INRD"s goal is to work toward data exchange on diskette.

Participation

The response to the formation of INRD has been positive. Members of the working committee have been regular in their attendance at meetings, and have reiterated their commitment to continue INRD activities. Parent organizations have provided facilities for meetings. Eleven libraries have provided inputs to the two INRD bulletins that have been published to date. However, the responsibility for the network should be taken by the national organization, and a coordinating body should be identified to take over this function. As resource sharing is essential for the development of a national information system, the members should be more outward looking and consider networking a part of the their professional duties.

Finance

Earlier networks planned in Bangladesh could not be made operational due to the lack of financial resources. INRD, however, commenced activities without external funding, and has been functioning with internal resources, with members bearing the costs. If networking is considered as an integral part of the activities of the libraries, a self–reliant network can be built on a cost sharing basis among the linked institutions. External resources may be solicited for expanding its activities, but a time will come when project funding will cease and the network will have to continue on its own. One way to resolve the issue of financial support is for each library to prevail on its organization to make a budgetary provision for networking. Cost saving, which may be achieved, for example, by participating in a cooperative acquisitions program, will more than compensate for the expenditure incurred on network programs.

CONCLUSION

Education aims to impart knowledge and makes good citizens. Libraries are the repositories of knowledge and form an integral part of education. Libraries have a long history, starting with the chained and closed-access libraries of earlier times to the present-day hybrid, digital, and virtual libraries that use the latest technology for provision of information through various services. Accordingly, librarians have also changed from storekeepers who were concerned with protection of books against theft, mutilation, and pilferage, to that of information officers, navigators, and cybrarians who find themselves in the vast ocean of reading material and are busy in satisfying their clients who want anytime and anywhere information.

Academic libraries are considered to be the nerve centres of academic institutions, and must support teaching, research, and other academic programmers. The situation in academic libraries of India is the same as that of academic libraries the world over; however, Indian libraries must provide maximum information with limited resources.

REFERENCES

1. Hussain, Rashid. Role of Information Communication Technology in Rural Development. Proceeding of the XXI National Seminar of IASLIC. 31st Dec. 2004 - 3rd Jan. 2005. Jadavpur University, Kolkata; pp.143-148.
2. Ibohal Singh, Charan and Lahiri (Ramansu). Library and Information Services in Rural Areas of Manipur. MALA. Rural Libraries in Manipur. 2003; pp18-30.
3. Jange, S, Sheriker, A. and Policegoudar, S.B. Exploring Information and Communication Technologies (ICT) for Rural Development and Security: India Perspectives. Proceeding of the

XXI National Seminar of IASLIC. 31st Dec. 2004 – 3rd Jan. 2005. Jadavpur University, Kolkata; pp 149 – 158. 388

4. Kumar, P.S.G. Integrated Information System Needed with Gram Panchayats as a Hub. IASLIC Bulletin. Vol. 45 (3), September 2000; pp. 97-104.

5. Kumaresen, S.C. and Chitra, Alosia. A Study on the Need for Rural Information Centres in the Villages of TamilNadu. Annals of Library and Information Studies, Vol.50 (4), December 2003; pp.137-145.

6. Lahkar, Narendra. Library Networks in India and the N.E India. Paper presented on the 2-Day Talk Cum – Seminar at Manipur University, 26-27th May, 2005.

7. Mahajan, Preeti. Information Support for Rural development: A Study of Punjab. Proceeding of the XXI National Seminar of IASLIC. 31st Dec. 2004 – 3rd Jan. 2005. Jadavpur University, Kolkata; pp.49-52.

8. Mukhopadhyay, Ananda Deb. Integrated Rural Development (IRD) and Information Support System (ISS). IASLIC Bulletin. Vol. 48(3), September 2003; pp. 131-140.

9. Sanajaoba Singh (P) and Premabati Devi (A). Information Needs and Seeking Behaviour of Users in the Rural Libraries of Manipur. MALA. Rural Libraries in Manipur. 2003; pp.1-7.

10. Henry, Carol ed. The Public Library Service. IFLA/UNESCO Guideline for Development. IFLA Publication p. 40.

11. Uddin, Md. Hanif. The Role of Rural Libraries in the Rural Development of Bangladesh. IASLIC Bulletin, Vol. 45(3), September 2000; pp.97-104.

12. Uttam,C. L. Importance of Government – to – Citizen and E-Governance Concept in Networking Programme of Govt. of Manipur. Paper presented on the 2-Day Talk – Cum – Seminar at Manipur University, 26-27th May, 2005.

13. Vijayakumar, M. et al. Community Information Service through Rural Library: A Case Study.Proceeding of the XXI National Seminar of IASLIC. 31st Dec. 2004 – 3rd Jan. 2005. JadavpurUniversity, Kolkata; pp.143-148.

14. Yapa, N.U.Utilization of ICT for LIS with Special Reference to SriLanka.

15. Debal C Kar, Parha Bhattacharya and Subrata Deb :Library Networking in India for Resources Sharing: Present Status and Prospects

9

Online Digital Collections and Content Management System through Omeka

Sukumar Mandal*

ABSTRACT

This paper highlights the content management system and online digital collections by using the omeka open source software. All the parameters are to be selected which is available in omeka databases both in admin as well as user interfaces. This research paper also explores the single window based interfaces icon for better management of content and online digital document. This research work can help the college libraries under the University of Burdwan because it can easily managed the unqualified dublin core metadata in different item types and their collection. Recall and precission is one of the core aspects in automated and digital library system and it optimosed through omeka software for information retrieval to the users as well as advanced users including teachers, students and researchers. Also managed the image file and their indexing in respective manner which available in omeka databases. The important questions is how to design

* Assistant Professor, The University of Burdwan, Burdwan-713104

the conetent management and digital document by the omeka software? All the data and parameters are to be selected on the basis of content management and digital recommendations for designing and developing the college libraries under the University of Burdwan.

Keywords : Omeka; Content management system; digital document and single window based interface

INTRODUCTION

Most of the academic libraries are highly involved in building institutional repositories of the institution's in different items like books, papers, theses, and other works which can be digitized or were 'born digital' (Kresh & Council on Library and Information Resources, 2007). Repositories are important in different insitutions because it can manage the open access resources for related with journals and other electronic resources. It is provides sophisticated search interface to find the digital resources which avaiable in this repositories. Institutional digital repositories can easily manage by the open harvesting tool like OAI-PMH which helps to access the open access documents and it also possible to search the specific resources from the particular repositories. It is fully support the metadata and search engines including Google Scholar, Yahoo! and Scirus can also use OAI-PMH to find these deep web resources (Koehler, 2006). With perpetuated ameliorations in book handling and presentation technologies such as optical character apperception and improvement of alternative depositories and business models, digital libraries are rapidly growing in popularity. (Tiwari, 2008). Just as libraries have ventured into audio and video amassments, so have digital libraries such as the Internet Archive (Ferguson, 2007). Web Content Management system is also an important aspect in online digital collections which helps the users of different departments in an effective and efficient way. Over the past few years the incresing of web resources of different organizations to publish and communicate the information via the web link. In this paper the important things is that the online digital collections is possible by content management system which can helps to create and publish the library resources. Advancements in the field of research and development has led to technologies such as; distributed computing, content management, data mining and processing, all of which fulfil a range of the users needs (Jean, 2011). The peregrinate from localised computing platforms to distributed web technologies has been caused by, among other factors, the take-up of commodity of different computer and network components predicated on more expeditious hardware and sophisticated software (Zhou; Dialani; Roure & Hall, 2003).

OBJECTIVES

The technological results, mainly in the area of Database Management and Information Retrieval, and as an application of these technologies are to the management of libraries. Sometime it has been used to denote a categorical application built to make accessible a concrete digital content. Thus, the important objectives are to be explained in the following ways:

- To explore the content management system and online digital collections through omeka;
- To find out the unqualified metadata managed by Dublin Core metadata standards;
- To explore the images upload in different file formats and displaying for both the interfaces and content and file;
- To highlights the different search techniques and search operators used in user interfaces for browsing and items collections.

DIGITAL COLLECTIONS

Digital amassments are no longer simply self-contained, single-purport entities constructed only to meet an immediate need (Barnes, 2004). Practitioners have come to agnize the potential of digital amassments to function as reusable components and it manage the different kinds of resources with the metadata plus fulltext library collections (Bishop; Van & Buttenfield, 2003). The academic library is the heart of insitutions because it can manage the both manual and machine related documents. It can easily create the virtual library both the users in campus and outside the campus (Chaudhuri & Parui, 2014). A good academic library accumulation manager considers not only near-term and proximate core users but withal the wider and more diverse audience of both current and future potential users (Witten; Bainbridge & Nichols, 2010). In culling items for print amassments, librarians follow selec-tion guidelines that have been proven to engender accumulations of broad, lasting worth and utility (Hou, 1983). Managers and implementers of digital amassments are expected to take the same approach. This designates that digitization project planners today must consider issues of long-term value, reusability, assiduousness, sustainability, interoperability, verification, and documentation. The National Science Substratum (NSF) has this explication on its web site for the Digital Library Initiative projects: Digital Libraries rudimentally store materials in electronic format and manipulate sizably voluminous accumulations of those materials efficaciously. Research is easily possible from the digital libraries through the Internet connectivity information systems, concentrating on how to develop the obligatory infrastructure to efficaciously mass-manipulate the information on the Net (NSF, 1999). The digital library is the accumulation of accommodations and the accumulation of information objects that support users in reveals the different information objects which available directly or indirectly via electronic/digital denotes (Leiner, 1998).

CONTENT MANAGEMENT SYSTEM

The World Wide Web has matured, so have people's prospects of their Web expe-riences. After becoming habituated in different web resources with what they can find and how to find it, Web visitors have commenced to expect more and timelier information from the Web sites they visit. Content management system is a bundled or stand-alone application to engender, deploy, manage and store content on Web pages (Fraser, 2002). Web content reveals the different items which including the text and embedded graphics, photos, video, audio, and code (e.g., for applications) that exhibits content or interacts with the utilizer. Content Management has many roles in today's emporium and is a paramount base for any website blogging, articles, news, description of products etc. Such systems of content management that provides the procedures and techniques to manage workflow in a collaborative environment. These techniques and procedures can be manual steps or an automated cascade. CMSs have been available since the tardy 1990s. CMSs are often used in different areas to run websites containing blogs, news, and shopping. Many corporate and marketing websites use CMSs (Arthur, 2006). CMSs typically aim to eschew the desideratum for hand coding, but may avail it for concrete elements or entire pages. Web CMS may catalog and index content, cull or assemble content at runtime, or distribute content to categorical visitors in a requested way, such as other languages (Kathuria, 2006). Web Content Management System's conventionally sanction client control over HyperText Markup Language - predicated content, files, documents, and Web hosting plans predicated on the system depth and the niche it accommodates.

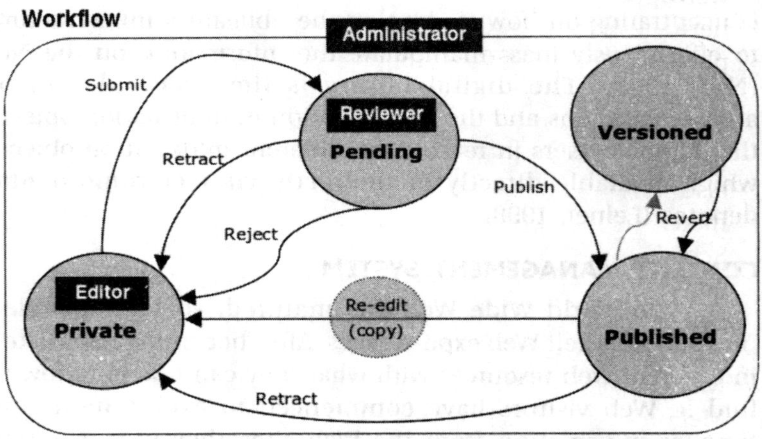

Fig. 1. Workflow of Content Management System

The workflow of content management system is also emphasizes both for general level users and advanced level patrons to manage the web documents and resources. The Figure – 1 is represents the workflow of CMS for the college libraries affiliated under the University of Burdwan which can easily manage the digital metadata by using the omeka. Simply content management system is the more sophisticated searching and browsing for building websites and managing web content

(Christianson; Cochran; Spohn & Ivan, 2009). It provides a set of integrated implements to avail technical and non-technical web publishers in the University to manage, engender and maintain websites and/or intranets and simply optate a pre-packaged theme for website, or engender a theme that's thoroughly customized to your own look and needs (Brampton, 2008). Therefore, the editors never publish the web contents from the live site and they only submit the content with file linking to the reviewer for the publication or rejects the resources which available in websites.

DEVELOPMENT OF DIGITAL COLLECTIONS AND CONTENT MANAGEMENT SYSTEM

Omeka (Table -1) is a open source content management system for online digital collections in college libraries. As a web application, it sanctions users to publish and exhibit cultural heritage objects, and elongate its functionality with themes and plugins. The most comprehensive and important institutional repository related softwares including Dspace, Eprints, Fedora and Omeka. But this research paper only select the omeka because it can manage both dublin core metadata with fulltext also. This software is used by the New York Public Library and many small museums and historical societies also. The Missouri School of Journalism uses Omeka to apportion their archive of 38,000 photographs from the Pictures of the Year International contest and it Developed by the Roy Rosenzweig Center for History and Incipient Media at George Mason University, Omeka was awarded by a technology collaboration award by the Andrew Mellon Substratum.

Table 1. Description on Omeka

Developer(s)	Roy Rosenzweig Center for History and New Media (CHNM) at George Mason University (GMU)
Written in	PHP
Operating system	Support both the Windows and Linux operating system
Type	Content Management System and online digital collections
License	GPL
Website	http://www.omeka.org/

Dashboard

Each and every content management system one option is important and this option known as dashboard. It is easily manage the present web contents and fulltext also. The recall and precision is also fulfill by using this tool because it can retrieve the right information in different search techniques like truncation or proximity search operators. Edit and modify is also possible from the admin interfaces and also manage the blog in college libraries. Real time search results is very sophisticated for the library websites. The Figure – 2 is represents the dashbaord in omeka to create and manage the important library resources both educational and administrative. Users can change the login and password as super user to create and maintain the college websites.

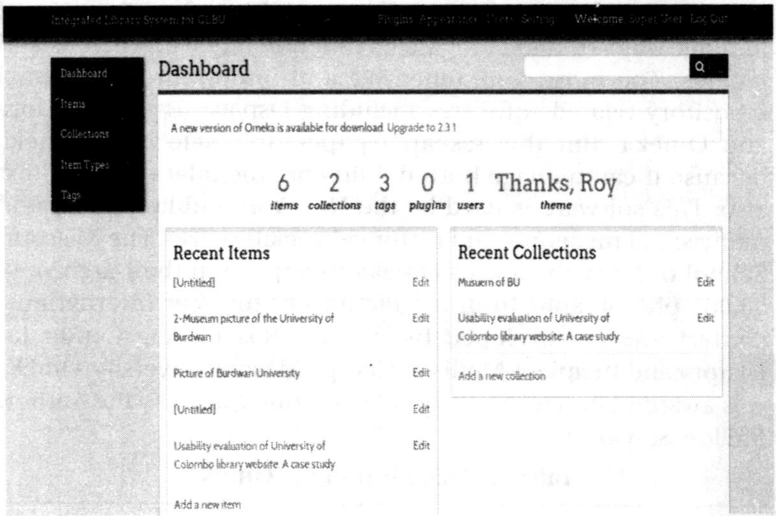

Fig. 2. Dashboard of Omeka

Items

Omeka managed the different types of metadata in respect of different formats. The Figure – 3 is represents the jpg file as well as pdf file in a single window based interface. Display the total items avaiable in one collection and it will helpful both for users as well as librarians.

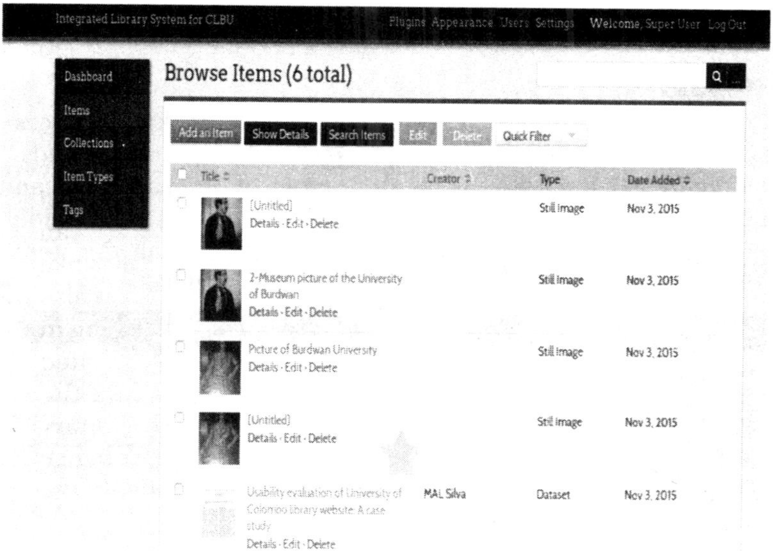

Fig. 3. Items interface of omeka

COLLECTIONS

Collection is one of the important concept in content management system and online digital collections. Items created under the collections and it consists of 15 dublin core elements metadata. Add items under each collection name because users can easily access the online resources. The Figure – 4 is represents the collections of omeka interface and here also add the new collection for the library as well as educational institutions.

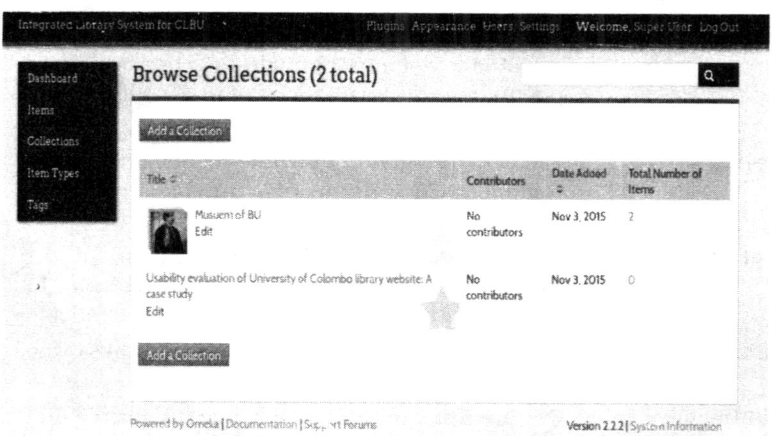

Fig. 4. Omeka collection interface

Item Types

There are 16 item types are default in omeka interfaces and here user can create new item types for their personal needs. The Figure – 5 is represents the item types of omeka which can managed the content as well as digital documents by using dublin core metadata unqualified standards and all the item type and their description represents in the Table -2.

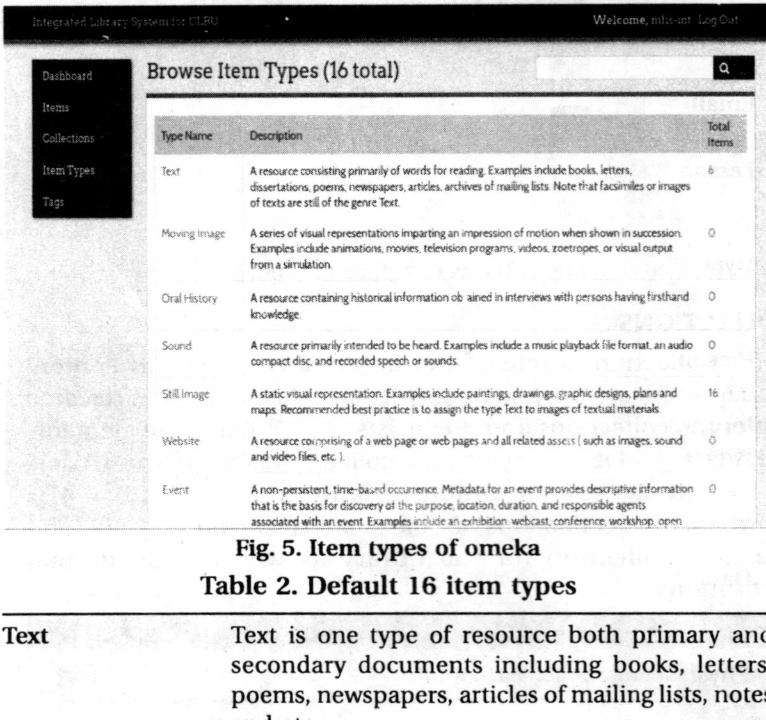

Fig. 5. Item types of omeka

Table 2. Default 16 item types

Text	Text is one type of resource both primary and secondary documents including books, letters, poems, newspapers, articles of mailing lists, notes and etc.
Moving Image	Visual representations of different documents with formats like animations, movies, television programs, videos and etc.
Oral History	A library related resource both historical and traditional information which obtained from the persons interviews.
Sound	Sound related resources like music, audio, video, speech and etc.
Still Image	Static representation of visual resource like

	drawings, graphics, maps, plans and text to the images of textual resources and documents.
Website	Website containing of different types resources by the different menues and sub-menues which publish the college websites with file formats such as images, sound and video files, etc.
Event	Metadata related with the non-persistent like webcast, workshop, seminar, conference, battle, exhibition, conference and etc. These can be manage in college libraries by using the omeka software.
Email	Textual information and file can be send to the college users from the library websites.
Lesson Plan	Learning resource can be access and manage by using this software with proper utilization and instruction to the students.
Hyperlink	Hyperlink can access the resources from the other Internet or references both the cited and citing documents.
Person	Individual or the peoples and students in college libraries.
Interactive Resource	Resource which interaction from the students to be easily understood, executed and read with experienced indifferent as pects like Web pages, applets, multimedia learning objects, chat services, or virtual reality environments.
Dataset	Data encoded in a defined structure. Examples include lists, tables, and databases. A dataset may be useful for direct machine processing.
Physical Object	An inanimate, three-dimensional object or substance. Note that digital representations of, or surrogates for, these objects should use Moving Image, Still Image, Text or one of the other types.
Service	A system that provides one or more functions. Examples include a photocopying service, a banking service, an authentication service, interlibrary loans, a Z39.50 or Web server.
Software	A computer program in source or compiled form. Examples include a C source file, MS-Windows .exe executable, or Perl script.

Tags

The browse tags panel displays all the tags associated with items in your archive, weighted by frequency used and user may sort all the tags by most popular (See Figure - 6), least popular, alphabetically, or by the tags most recently added to items. Clicking on a tag will take you to the items/browse page, displaying only items tagged with the tag clicked by the user. Editing a tag allows you to rename a tag across all instances that it occurs. Choose a tag that wish to edit, and rename it in the text box and Click "Save Changes" and your tag will be saved with its new name. Deleting a tag removes all occurrences of that tag across all items, for all users. To completely delete a tag choose the tag user wish to delete from the select menu and click "Delete tag" button. That tag will then be permanently deleted from the installation. ags are keywords or phrases that describe a piece of data. They are non-hierarchical labels that classify your content so that it is easily found and manage the tags, sign into the Omeka admin panel and select Tags from the left-hand navigation bar. This displays all the tags associated with items in your archive. You may edit tags, delete tags, view items associated with individual tags, and sort tags.

Fig. 6. Tags in omeka

MANAGED UNQUALIFIED METADATA

The Dublin Core Extended plugin adds the full set of Dublin Core properties to the existing Dublin Core element set, including element refinements and supplemental elements. contribute to a movement that is helping to standardize data about digital objects. While there are different standards available, the Dublin Core Metadata Initiative is the most widely adopted and offers users the greatest flexibility. Temporal topic may be a named period, date, or date range. A jurisdiction may be a named administrative entity or a geographic place to which the resource applies. Recommended best practice is to use a controlled vocabulary such as the Thesaurus of Geographic Names [TGN]. Where appropriate, named places or time periods can be used in preference to numeric identifiers such as sets of coordinates or date ranges.

Table 3. 15 Unqualified Dublin Core metadata elements and their description

Title	A name given to the resource.
Subject	The topic of the resource.
Description	An account of the resource.
Creator	An entity primarily responsible for making the resource.
Source	A related resource from which the described resource is derived.
Publisher	An entity responsible for making the resource available.
Date	A point or period of time associated with an event in the lifecycle of the resource.
Contributor	An entity responsible for making contributions to the resource.
Rights	Information about rights held in and over the resource.
Relation	A related resource.
Format	The file format, physical medium, or dimensions of the resource.
Language	A language of the resource.
Type	The nature or genre of the resource.
Identifier	An unambiguous reference to the resource within a given context.

Coverage	The spatial or temporal topic of the resource, the spatial applicability of the resource, or the jurisdiction under which the resource is relevant.

The Figure – 7 represents the Dublin Core interface in omeka and it can managed the metadata for the item types and their collection. It can easily managed the content data and digital data both the admin as well user interfaces.

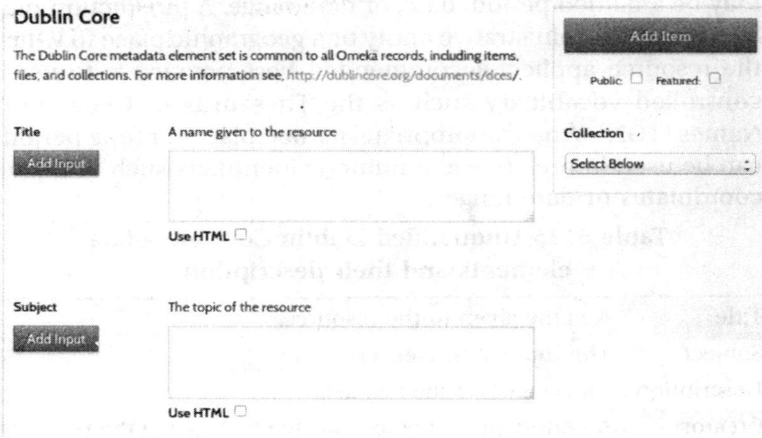

Fig. 7. Dublin core metadta schema interface in omeka

SINGLE WINDOW INTERFACE ON UBUNTU

This is one of the important concept explores by this paper and here the Figure – 8 represents the single window based interface in omeka on Ubuntu 14.04. Create desktop icon through ubuntu desktop script and click on the icon for access the omeka interface for the users as well as library professionals towards next level automated and digital library system. Search facilities are available in omeka interfaces such as advanced search and simple search and browse the items is respects of collections which create by the omeka users (Super or admin). In this way users can collect their relevant information in different formats for the different documents types and multiple document interface (MDI) is a graphical user interface in which multiple windows reside under a single parent window.

Fig. 8. Omeka single window interface icon

CONCLUSION

Content management system and online digital collections is one of the important tasks in automated and digital library system for the college libraries under the University of Burdwan and not in college libraries this research work also apply in any other institutions (Academic, public and research libraries). The iso framework is easily managed the content and digital resources for the users as well as library professionals. Unqualified metadata is managed by omeka for designing and developing the content related document in the area of content management system cluster.The software is not dependent on local operating system, so it doesn't matter if you use a Mac, PC or Linux. And when it comes to hosting a Joomla site, you can choose a host that uses the Apache server (which is usually run on the Linux operating system) or Windows IIS. The majority of omeka sites are hosted on Linux powered servers. All the unqualified Dublin core metadata are to be easily managed, edit and delete the content related resources after global configuration for setup the metadata structure in different domain specific cluster. Obviously, this research work crafted or extend in any type or size of a library because it support web-enabled server (Apache) and access all the users under the campus of college libraries under the University of Burdwan.

REFERENCES

1. Arthur, M. H. (2006). Expanding a digital content management system: For the growing digital media enterprise. Amsterdam: Elsevier Focal Press.
2. Barnes, S. J. (2004). Becoming a digital library. New York: Marcel Dekker.
3. Bishop, A. P., Van, H. N. A., & Buttenfield, B. P. (2003). Digital library use: Social practice in design and evaluation. Cambridge, Mass: MIT Press.
4. Brampton, M. (2008). PHP5 CMS framework development: Expert insight and practical guidance to creating an efficient, flexible and robust framework for a PHP5-based content management system. Birmingham, U.K: Packt Pub.
5. Chaudhuri, B. B., & Parui, S. K. (2014). Advances in Digital Document Processing and Retrieval.
6. Christianson, C., Cochran, J., Spohn, J. L., & Ivan, B. (2009). ASP.NET 3.5 content management system development: Build, manage, and extend your own content management system. Birmingham, U.K: Packt Pub.
7. Ferguson, A. (2007). Creating content management systems in Java. Boston, Mass: Charles River Media.
8. Fraser, S. R. G. (2002). Real-world ASP. Net: Building a content management system. Berkeley, Calif: Apress.
9. Hou, H. S. (1983). Digital document processing. New York: Wiley.
10. Jean, G. (2011). Digital Library. New Delhi: World Technologies.
11. Kathuria, G. (2006). Web content management with Documentum: Set up, design, develop, and deploy Documentum applications : concise, practical information on Documentum Web Content Management to get the most from this system. Birmingham, UK: Packt Pub.
12. Koehler, AEC (2006). Some Thoughts on the Meaning of Open Access for University Library Technical Services Serials Review Vol. 32 (1), p. 17.

13. Kresh, D., & Council on Library and Information Resources. (2007). The whole digital library handbook. Chicago: American Library Association.

14. Leiner, B.M. (1998), "The NCSTRL approach to open architecture for the confederated digital library", D-Lib Magazine , available at: www.dlib.org/dlib/december98/leiner/12leiner.html

15. National Science Foundation (1999). Digital Libraries Initiative: Available Research, US Federal Government, available at: http://dli2.nsf.gov/dlione.

16. Tiwari, P. (2008). Digital library. New Delhi: A P H Publishing Corporation.

17. Witten, I. H., Bainbridge, D., & Nichols, D. M. (2010). How to build a digital library. Burlington, MA: Morgan Kaufmann Publishers.

18. Zhou, J., Dialani, V., Roure, D. D. & Hall, W. (2003), A semantic search algorithm for peer-to-peer open hypermedia systems, in 'The First Work- shop on Semantics in Peer-to-Peer and Grid Computing', pp. 43–54.

10

From Cloud to Fog Paradigm and Security Issues

Sudhir Kumar Jena*

ABSTRACT

Fog Computing is a paradigm that extends cloud computing and services to the edge of the network. Similar to Cloud, Fog provides data, compute, storage, and application services to end-users. In this article, we elaborate the motivation and advantages of Fog computing, and analyze its applications in a series of real scenarios, such as Smart Grid, smart traffic lights in vehicular networks and software defined networks. We discuss the state-of-the-art of Fog computing and similar work under the same umbrella. Security and privacy issues are further disclosed according to current Fog computing paradigm. As an example, we study a typical attack, man-in-the-middle attack, for the discussion of security in Fog computing. We investigate the stealthy features of this attack by examining its CPU and memory consumption on Fog device.

Keywords : Fog Computing, Cloud Computing, Software, Networks.

* Librarian, IIM Shillong

INTRODUCTION

In today's world, the way to store and retrieve or access personal as well as other information has captured a massive revolution. Carrying the personal/official data on a physical device has become outdated with the rapid growth of network and users can connect virtually to data from anywhere and anyplace. That how cloud computing has emerged and widespread to meet the demand of latency, reliability, security and efficiency.

From the past few years, Cloud computing has served abundant opportunities for business by providing users a wide length of computing services. It also overcomes platform dependency problems with no software installation on user side which makes enterprise applications mobile and collaborative. The pay only for service used model becomes an economical substitute for managing and be responsible for data centers to web applications and batch processing users. With the less maintenance and cost based on service usage, cloud computing's layered architecture allows the client to purchase services at different levels such as IaaS, PaaS and SaaS, depending upon their customer requirements. It permits location independence facility as users can access these services anywhere with an internet connection and a web browser. But the problem is too much data is going to strike in coming years.

Increase in the huge number of devices getting connected to the network is mainly by two sources: Devices and sensors or actuators. In IoT, devices assemble and communicate information directly with each other via internet and the cloud manages to collect record and analyze data blocks. But the 'things or devices' which are producing massive amount of data is blowing out day-to-day that needs to be treated, managed, analyzed and stocked at cloud. For example, Boeing 787 creates half a terabyte of data/flight says Virgin Atlantic. According to statistics: Back in 2008, there are already more objects connected to the Internet than people. This year, 4.9 billion connected things. The number will reach or exceed 50 billion by 2020. The outbreak in the number of devices/person is interpreted by the generation of mobile devices like mobile phones and tablets.

From, 30.7 % of IoT devices found in Healthcare and 69.7% of IoT devices found elsewhere (Business, Manufacturing, Retail, Security and Transportation) and this shows the constantly growing of loads of data.From, IoT devices generate data constantly, and often analysis must be very rapid. Handling the volume, variety, and velocity of IoT data requires a new computing model. The main requirements are to:

Minimize Latency : Analyzing data close to the device that collected the data can make the difference between averting disaster and a cascading system failure.

Conserve Network Bandwidth : Offshore oilrigs generate 500 GB of data weekly. It is not practical to transport vast amounts of data from thousands or hundreds of thousands of edge devices to the cloud. Nor is it necessary, because many critical analyses do not require cloud-scale processing and storage.

Address Security Concerns : IoT data needs to be protected both in transit and at rest. This requires monitoring and automated response across the entire attack continuum: before, during, and after.

Operate Reliably : IoT data is increasingly used for decisions affecting citizen safety and critical infrastructure. The integrity and availability of the infrastructure and data cannot be in question.

Move Data to the best Place for Processing : Which place is best depends partly on how quickly a decision is needed. Extremely time-sensitive decisions should be made closer to the things producing and acting on the data. In contrast, big data analytics on historical data needs the computing and storage resources of the cloud.

WHAT IS FOG COMPUTING?

The term "Fog Computing" was introduced by the Cisco Systems as new model to ease wireless data transfer to distributed devices in the Internet of Things (IoT) network paradigm. According to Bonomi et al., the rationale for coining this term to identify this model is that fog is nothing but cloud that is closer to the ground. Hence cloud computing carried out closer to the end users' networks is thus identified as fog computing.

Thus fog computing can provide better quality of service in terms of delay, power consumption, reduced data traffic over the Internet etc . The main feature of fog computing is its ability to support applications that require low latency, location awareness and mobility. This ability is made possible by the fact that the fog computing systems are deployed very close to the end users in a widely distributed manner.

Traditional cloud computing architectures do not meet all of these requirements. The prevailing approach moving all data from the network edge to the data center for processing adds latency. Traffic from thousands of devices soon outstrips bandwidth capacity. In addition, cloud servers communicate only with IP, not the countless other protocols used by IoT devices. The ideal place to analyze most IoT data is near the devices that produce and act on that data. We call it Fog computing.

This "fog computing" concept has been launch as a bridge linking IoT devices and far off data centers. IoT devices are producing large amount of data that is necessary to be processed. With this model, by treating and outlining the data to reduce quantity, improve value and purpose by processing some of by computation resources at the edge.

WHY DO WE NEED FOG?

In the past few years, Cloud computing has provided many opportunities for enterprises by offering their customers arrange of computing services. Current "pay-as-you-go" Cloud computing model becomes an efficient alternative to owning and managing private data centres for customers facing Web applications and batch processing. Cloud computing frees the enterprises and their end users from the specification of many details, such as storage resources, computation limitation and network communication cost. However, this bliss becomes a problem for latency-sensitive applications, which require nodes in the vicinity to meet their delay requirements. When techniques and devices of IoT are getting more involved in people's life, current Cloud computing paradigm can hardly satisfy their requirements of mobility support, location awareness and low latency.

Fog computing is proposed to address the above problem. As Fog computing is implemented at the edge of the network, it provides low latency, location awareness, and improves quality-of-services (QoS) for streaming and real time applications. Typical examples include industrial automation, transportation, and networks of sensors and actuators. Moreover, this new infrastructure supports heterogeneity as Fog devices include end-user devices, access points, edge routers and switches. The Fog paradigm is well positioned for real time big data analytics, supports densely distributed data collection points, and provides advantages in entertainment, advertising, personal computing and other applications.

CLOUD Vs FOG

From the above discussion, it can be seen that technically fog computing is very much similar to cloud computing in the sense that both are made up of virtual systems providing the flexibility of on demand provisioning of compute, storage and network resources. But compared to cloud, fog is implemented very close to the end users In this section, we take an in depth look at the similarities and dissimilarities of these two technologies with respect to the demands of the emerging trends in networking. Table 1 summarizes the results of the comparison. From Table 1, it can be seen that Cloud Computing characteristics have very severe limitations with respect to quality of service demanded by real time applications requiring almost immediate action by the server. The detailed explanation on the comparison with respect to their impacts is given below.

Table 1. Cloud Computing vs Fog Computing

Requirement	Cloud Computing	Fog Computing
Latency	High	Low
Delay Jitter	High	Very Low
Location of server nodes	Within the Internet	At the edge of the local network

Distance between the client and server	Multiple Hops	One hop
Security	Undefined	Can be defined
Attack on data enroute	High probability	Very low probability
Location awareness	No	Yes
Geographical distribution	Centralized	Distributed
No. of server nodes	Few	Very Large
Support for Mobility	Limited	Supported
Real time interactions	Supported	Supported
Type of last mile connectivity	Leased line	Wireless

MOTIVATION AND RELATED WORK

The emerging technologies: Cloud and Fog computing are in support to the IoT. Cloud Computing enables researchers and businesses to use and maintain many resources remotely, reliably and at a low cost. The IoT employs a large number of embedded devices, like sensors and actuators that generate big data which in turn requires complex computations to extract knowledge. Therefore, the storage and computing resources of the cloud present the best choice for the IoT to store and process big data. Employing Cloud Computing for the IoT is not an easy task due to the following challenges;

Synchronization : Synchronization between different cloud vendors presents a challenge to provide real-time services since services are built on top of various cloud platforms.

Standardization : Standardizing CC also presents a significant challenge for IoT cloud-based services due having to interoperate with the various vendors.

Balancing : Making a balance between general cloud service environments and IoT requirements presents another challenge due to the differences in infrastructure.

Reliability : Security of IoT cloud-based services presents another challenge due to the differences in the security mechanisms between the IoT devices and the cloud platforms.

Management : Managing CC and IoT systems is also a challenging factor due to the fact that both have different resources and components.

Enhancement : Validating IoT cloud-based services is necessary to ensure providing good services that meet the customers' expectations.

The applications of Fog are as multiple as the IoT itself. Monitoring or analyzing data in real-time from network-connected things and initiating an action are something similar they have. Fog Computing is a highly virtualized platform that provides networking services between end devices and traditional Cloud Computing Data Centers, but not exclusively located at the edge of network.

Fog computing can serve as an optimal choice for the IoT designers for the following features.

Location : Fog resources are positioned between smart objects and the cloud data-centers; thus, providing better delay performance.

Distribution : Since fog computing is based on "micro" centers with limited storage, processing and communication capabilities compared to the cloud, it is possible to deploy many such "micro" centers closer to the end-users as their cost is typically a small fraction compared to cloud data-centers.

Scalability : Fog allows IoT systems to be more scalable such that as the number of end-users increase, the number of deployed "micro" fog centers can increase to cope with the increasing load. Such an increase cannot be achieved by the cloud because the deployment of new data-centers is cost prohibitive.

Density of devices : Fog helps to provide resilient and replicated services.

Mobility support : Fog resources act as a "mobile" cloud as it is located close to the end-users.

Real-time : Fog has the potential to provide better performance for real-time interactive services.

Standardization : Fog resources can interoperate with various cloud provides.

On the fly analysis : Fog resources can perform data aggregation to send partially processed data as opposed to raw data to the cloud data-centers for further processing.

Therefore, fog computing has the potential to increase the overall performance of ICT applications as it tries to perform part of high level services which are offered by cloud inside the local resources. Actually what happens in Fog and Cloud Computing, below points helps in understanding:

FOG NODES

- Receive feeds from IoT devices using any protocol, in real time.
- Run IoT-enabled applications for real-time control and analytics, with millisecond response time.
- Provide transient storage often.
- Send periodic data summaries to the cloud.

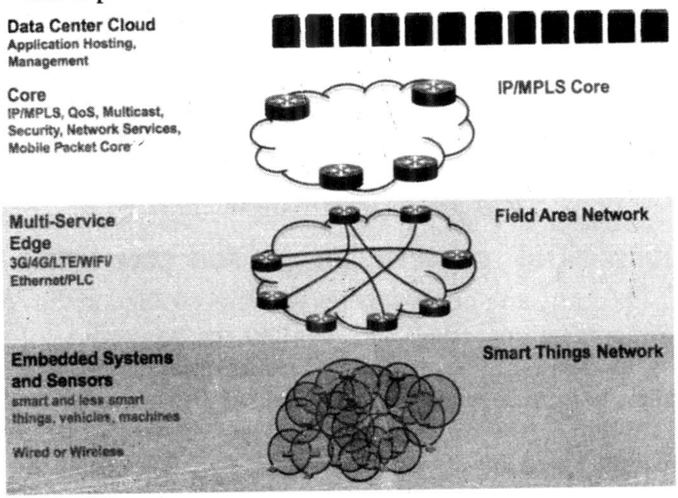

Fig. 1. Cisco Fog and IoT Distributed Architecture

PROPOSED CLOUD TO FOG (C2F) COMPUTING MODEL

U-Healthcare monitoring finds a way in the Fog. The Architecture of a Fog and IoT-based real-time u-healthcare monitoring which can be used in smart hospitals or home is shown in Figure 2. There are 4 tiers in which this architecture gives reason of moving from cloud to fog and how it benefits the healthcare monitoring ubiquitously.

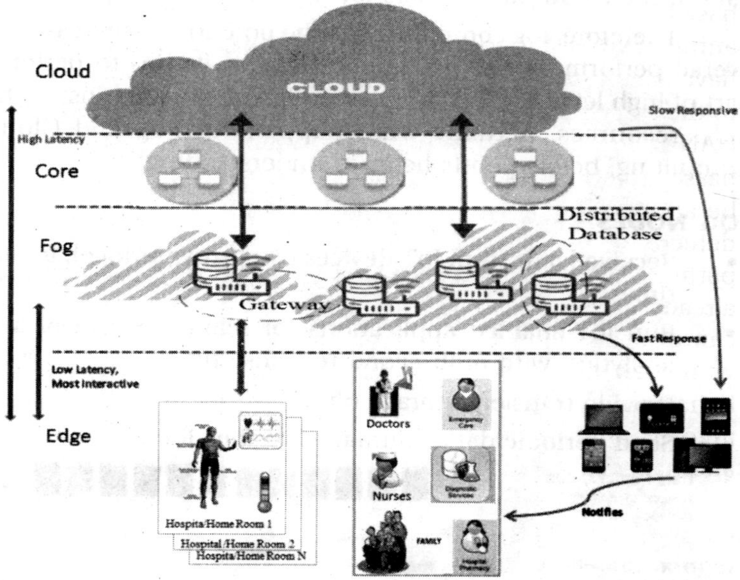

Fig. 2. C2F Computing and IoT Based Architecture for Real-time U-Healthcare Monitoring

SECURITY AND PRIVACY ISSUES IN FOG COMPUTING

Security and privacy issues were not studied in the context of fog computing. They were studied in the context of smart grids and machine-to-machine communications. There are security solutions for Cloud computing. However, they may not suit for Fog computing because Fog devices work at the edge of networks. The working surroundings of Fog devices will face with many threats which do not exist in well managed Cloud. In this section, we discuss the security and privacy issues in Fog Computing.

The main security issues are authentication at different levels of gateways as well as (in case of smart grids) at the smart meters installed in the consumer's home. Each smart meter and smart appliance has an IP address. A malicious user can either tamper with its own smart meter, report false readings, or spoof IP addresses. There are some solutions for the authentication problem. The work elaborated public key infrastructure (PKI) based solutions which involve multicast authentication. Some authentication techniques using Diffie-Hellman key exchange have been discussed in Smart meters encrypt the data and send to the Fog device, such as a home-area network (HAN) gateway. HAN then decrypts the data, aggregates the results and then passes them forward. Intrusion detection techniques can also be applied in Fog computing. Intrusion in smart grids can be detected using either a signature-based method in which the patterns of behaviour are observed and checked against an already existing database of possible misbehaviours. Intrusion can also be captured by using an anomaly-based method in which an observed behaviour is compared with expected behaviour to check if there is a deviation. The work develops an algorithm that monitors power flow results and detects anomalies in the input values that could have been modified by attacks. The algorithm detects intrusion by using principal component analysis to separate power flow variability into regular and irregular subspaces.

CONCLUSIONS AND FUTURE WORK

It is quite apparent that Cloud to Fog computing is delivering more effectively compared to cloud by meeting present requirements of emerging models that require quick processing with fewer delay. They both co-exist, serving two different sectors and complementing each other wherever required. From the above analysis, it can be seen that fog computing performs better than cloud computing in meeting the demands of the emerging paradigms. But fog computing cannot totally replace cloud computing as it will still be preferred for high end batch processing jobs that are very common in the business world. Hence it can be concluded that fog computing and cloud computing will complement each other while having their own advantages and disadvantages. Fog computing advantages for services in several domains, and provide the analysis of the state-of-the art and security issues in current paradigm

Future work will expand on the Fog computing paradigm in Smart Grid. In this scenario, two models for Fog devices can be developed. Independent Fog devices consult directly with the Cloud for periodic updates on price and demands, while interconnected Fog devices may consult each other, and create coalitions for further enhancements.

REFERENCES

1. Dave, E. (2011), The internet of things how the next evolution of the internet is changing everything. Technical report, CISCO IBSG.
2. Bonomi, F. (2011).Connected vehicles, the internet of things, and fog computing. in The Eighth ACM International Workshop on Vehicular Inter-Networking (VANET), Las Vegas, USA.
3. Cisco (2014).Cisco delivers vision of fog computing to accelerate value from billions of connected devices. Cisco, Tech. Rep.,.
4. Modi, C., Patel,D., Borisaniya, B., Patel, H., Patel, A. and M. Rajarajan (2013). Asurvey of intrusion detection techniques in cloud. Journal of Networkand Computer Applications, vol. 36, no. 1, pp. 42–57.
5. Bonomi, F., Milito, R., Zhu, J. and Addepalli, S. (2012), Fog computing and its role in the internet of things," in Proceedings of the First Edition ofthe MCC Workshop on Mobile Cloud Computing, ser. MCC'12. ACM,, pp. 13–16.
6. Madsen, H:, Albeanu, G., Burtschy, B. and Popentiu-Vladicescu, F.(2013). Reliability in the utility computing era: Towards reliable fog computing in Systems, Signals and Image Processing (IWSSIP), 2013 20thInternational Conference on, pp. 43–46.
7. Valenzuela, J., Wang, J.,and N. Bissinger, N. (2013). Real-time intrusion detection in power system operations, Power Systems, IEEE Transactions on,vol. 28, no. 2, pp. 1052–1062
8. Zhu, J., Chan, D., Prabhu, M., Natarajan, P., Hu, H., and Bonomi, F. (2013). Improving web sites Performance using edge servers in fog computing architecture. in Service Oriented System Engineering (SOSE), 2013IEEE 7th International Symposium on, pp. 320–323.
9. Kirkpatrick, K.(2013). Software-defined networking. Commun. ACM, vol. 56, no. 9, pp. 16–19,
10. Liu, K., Ng, J., Lee, V., Son, V. and Stojmenovic, I. (2014).

Cooperative datadissemination in hybrid ehicular networks: Vanet as a software defined network. Submitted for publication.

11. Armbrust, M., Fox, A., Griffith, R., Joseph, A.D., Katz, R.A., Konwinski, G. Lee, D. Patterson, A.,Rabkin, Stoica, I, and Zaharia, M.(2010), A view of cloud computing. Commun. ACM, vol. 53, no. 4, pp. 50–58.
12. Lu, R., Li, X., Liang, X. Shen, X.,and Lin, X. (2011). Grs: The green, reliability, and security of emerging machine to machine communications.Communications Magazine, IEEE, vol. 49, no. 4, pp. 28–35..
13. Maharjan, S., Zhu, Q., Zhang, Y., S. Gjessing, S., and Basar, T. (2013). Dependable demand response management in the smart grid: A stackelberg game approach," Smart Grid, IEEE Transactions on, vol. 4, no. 1, pp. 120– 132.
14. Luo,T., Tan, H.P,and T. Quek, T. (2012). Sensor open flow: Enabling software definedwireless Sensor networks, Communications Letters, IEEE, vol. 16, no. 11, pp. 1896–1899.
15. Nishio, T.,Shinkuma, R.,Takahashi, T. and Mandayam, N.B. (2013). Service oriented heterogeneous resource sharing for optimizing service latency in mobile cloud. in Proceedings of the First International Workshop on Mobile Cloud Computing and Networking, ser. MobileCloud'13. ACM, pp. 19–26.
16. Wang, W. and Z. Lu, Z. (2013). Survey cyber security in the smart grid: Survey and challenges. Comput. Netw., vol. 57, no. 5, pp. 1344–1371.
17. Wikipedia. (2014). Hooking, what is hooking? [Online]. Available: http://en.wikipedia.org/wiki/Hooking
18. Law, Y.W.,Palaniswami, M., Kounga, G.and A. Lo, A. (2013). Wake: Key Management cheme for wide-area measurement systems in smart grid. Communications Magazine, IEEE, vol. 51, no. 1, pp. 34–41.
19. Daraghmi, Y., Yi, C.W.,and I. Stojmenovic, I. (2013).Forwarding methods in data dissemination and routing protocols for vehicular ad hoc networks. Network, IEEE, vol. 27, no. 6, pp. 74–79.
20. Fadlullah, Z., Fouda, M., Kato, N., Takeuchi, A.,Iwasaki, N. and Nozaki, Y, (2011). Toward intelligent machine-to-machine communications in smart grid. Communications Magazine, IEEE, vol. 49, no. 4, pp. 60–65.
21. Fadlullah, Z., Quan, D., Kato, N.and I. Stojmenovic, I (2014). Gtes: An optimized game-theoretic demand-side management scheme for smart grid. SystemsJournal, IEEE, vol. 8, no. 2, pp. 588–597.

11

Changing Expectations and Perception of Technical Library Users

Prof. K. C. Das*

ABSTRACT

The article highlights about the changing expectations and perceptions of technical library users.Users' service desires are constantly changing under the spur of technological influence. In this article it is stated that how technical institution libraries are quite advanced and are using a lot of web based services for their users and trying to fulfill their expectations and changing needs. The article also highlights how these libraries have responded to users' expectations and their changing needs.

Keywords : Users Perception, Expectations, Changing Needs, Trends in Technical libraries

INTRODUCTION

The quick advancement of technological development congruent with modern information communication Technologies (ICT) in modern-day information society have

* Head, DLIS, Utkal University, Bhubaneswar-751004

rightly ushered the academic organizations. The capacity to manage both conventional and electronic resources effectively keeping pace with the changing information infrastructure and the changing needs of users' community.

Library and information service providers in this digital era are taking keen interest for understanding and gathering the changing needs of their users. In a period of shrinking budget, meeting users' requirement and satisfaction in enhancement of various resources and services have become vital for libraries to keep up to changes as user needs change. Also, libraries that comprehend the needs of their user base cannot just work better to address those needs, however can likewise advertise their services in a more viable design. Quick changes in library services and operations request for inward institutional responsibility and evaluation desires by outside certifying agencies have helped further advancement and application of user studies inside academic libraries amid the previous decades (Shafique et al, 2012).

According to (Durmaz, 2007) "Change will occur in organizations and for whatever reason; organizations need to change in order to survive and to be effective in the ever-changing technological environment". On the other hand, (Troll, 2002, p.99) has stated "academic libraries are changing in light of changes in the learning and research environment and changes in the behaviour of library users".

Technical libraries are challenged to adapt to this phase of information scattering and access. Library administrators feel constrained to act in response to the changing needs and expectations of users, and at times, are influenced by university and college managers to record for their uses and show the results they attain to (Nyamache et al, 2012). Whereas (Troll, 2002) expressed, why libraries are changing on the off chance that we are to clarify moving examples of library utilization, imagine the course of our evolutionary way, and win or support help for the changing bearings of academic libraries. Academic libraries must demonstrate the worth they give to the academic communities.

Technical libraries are now facing striking challenges from

one another as they are different from the past. The increasing of deficit budgets and changing technology have made significant impacts virtually on every library in some way or other. The changes that are occurring in technology, in research, teaching and learning have created a very different context for the missions of engineering and other technical college libraries. This scenario creates a challenge for libraries and librarians to respond to change in proactive and visionary ways.

Due to the above factors presently, Indian technical library management system is facing various challenges. Some of them are listed below:

- New roles and responsibilities
- Impact of IT
- Increased and diversified users information thrust and need
- Demand for quality based library and information products and services
- Development of Information Infrastructure
- Need for web based services
- Timely delivery of information materials to users
- Philosophy of information @door
- Concept of 24 hours and 7days service
- Responsiveness and dynamism in library system
- Creation of culture for creativity
- New tools and techniques of information handling
- Need for effective and efficient users interface
- Effective monitoring and feedback system
- Resources crunch
- Resource generation
- New electronic information environment
- Marketing of library and information products and services
- Users information behavior and reading habits
- Explosive growth of electronic information

- Unprecedented production of printed publications
- Need for Interaction with external environment
- Need to develop sustainable collection building strategy
- Need to create specialized database creation
- Increased cost of information materials
- Diversity of programs
- Emerging thrust areas
- Customers care
- Library networking and networks (Harish Chandra, 2004).

EXPECTATIONS

Expectations are "desires or wants of consumers, i.e., what they feel a service provider should offer rather than would offer" (Parasuraman, et al., 1988, p. 17). Several researchers such as Heath & Cook, (2003); and Shi, Holahan&Jurkat, (2004) have agreed that expectations serve as reference point which focuses in users' assessment.

However, Zeithaml, Berry and Parasuraman (1993) in another study have pointed out that user's desires are focused around the past experiences, informal interchanges, clear and undercover services guaranteed by an association. What's more, the coveted desires ought to additionally base on continuing service intensifiers and personal needs.

According to Berry (1995), there are eleven approaches to listen the users. These are value-based reviews, mystery shopping, new declining and lost client reviews, center gathering meetings, client advisory boards, service surveys, client complaint, remark, request capture, aggregate business studies, representative field reporting, employee surveys and service operating information capture (Cook, Heath, Thompson, & Thompson, 2001).

On the other hand, they reflect expected execution. Users have a tendency to hold expectations that can be considered really basic. Most users want quick execution and that assurances given are kept. Users desire a quality service, which should be given in a satisfying and friendly way.

PERCEPTION

Psychological investigation of human behaviour began with the study of perception by Wielheim Wundh in Germany in 1879. Since that time it has been significant in understanding human behaviour.The important revelation is that no two people experience and interpret sensations, situations, or their own feelings the same way. Perception is the way we all interpret our experiences. It is a marvelous and difficult part of human behaviour; librarians must realize that all individuals have differing perceptions.

The Chinese philosopher Lao-tzu said, "Knowing others are wisdom, knowing yourself is enlightenment."Each one of us perceives the world around us in different ways. It is our perception of that reality which shapes and directs our behaviour. For example, if one person on a hillside perceives that it is cold, he will reach for his sweater. On the other hand, if the person standing next to him perceives that it is warm, he will remove his sweater. Similarly, choose a film that you have seen recently and which you particularly enjoyed. Now, find a friend or colleague who has seen the same film and hated it.

- Thus, it is clear that human behaviour is a function of the way in which we perceive the world around us and how we perceive other people and-events in that world.
- We often find ourselves unable to understand other people's behaviour.
- To understand each other's behaviour, we should be able to understand each other's perceptions.
- Therefore, it can be said that if we wish to improve our understanding of others, we must first have a well-developed knowledge of ourselves - our strengths, our preferences, our weaknesses and our biases.

What is Perception?

Perception may be defined as the dynamic psychological process responsible for attending to, organising and interpreting sensory data. It is a process by which individuals organize and interpret their sensory impressions in order to give meaning to their environment.

Why is it Important?

Because people's behavior is based on their perception of what reality is, not on reality itself? The world that is perceived is the world that is behaviorally important.

Factors Influencing Perception

a. The Perceiver – attitudes, motives, interests, experiences, expectations

b. The Target – novelty, motions, sounds, size, background, proximity, similarity

c. The Situation – time, work setting, social situation

User's service desires

Users service desires fall into two classes: (1) service as a finished result or conclusion that includes unwavering quality or the capacity to perform a promised service both reliably and precisely; and (2) service process, which includes of the following dimensions statement (the capability of staff to convey on a high level of trust and confidence based on knowledge and compassion) responsiveness (a demonstrated ability to help users and give quick service), concern (giving, caring, individualized regard for users), and tangibles (the subsistence of physical facilities, the measure of equipment and staff, and the level of communication that be presents between the service provider and its users). Each one measurement of expectations is liable to include two service levels. The first is the wanted service level or what the users wants to get a mix of what can and ought to be. The second speaks to the satisfactory administration level-that level of service a user determines satisfactory (Cooper et al, 1998).

TECHNICAL LIBRARY USERS AND THEIR EXPECTATIONS

The understanding of users' desires and gathering those desires is the main way for libraries to hold their users. Library ought not to work altogether separation from its users' desires. Libraries leaders ought to know the users' desires to enhance the nature of services offered (Scott, 1992). Desires of users have changed Tech-clever new era requests: Quality, Rate and Atmosphere. Users oblige distinctive services; thus librarians are relied upon to give an assortment of services to them. Indeed inside one sort of library, users will request distinctive services. The services requested are not static, as users' necessities are dynamic, obliging diverse services at distinctive times. Subsequently, librarians must perceive that, their essential item is the users' experience. The need to create new service models that can help live up to users' changing desires in ways that include genuine esteem and store their role in the educational course of action gets to be certain. Fundamentally library professionals ought to figure out how to keep users fulfillment up by giving a top score user service. In the expressions of Kadiri (2000), there is the requirement for academic libraries to reappraise their service delivery ability as the librarian is equipped for framing a scaffold in the middle of students and teachers.

Akintola and Olayiwola (2004) stated that libraries must comprehend the progressive change and develop a method of connecting hierarchical structure to effectively meet users' needs. Library staffs are continually challenged to keep up to date with variety of new sources of information, databases, and search engines in addition to becoming more knowledgeable and aware of the Library's own vast collections".

Expectations of users from Library

Expectations are the standards upon which a service provider's performance should be judged. They reflect expected execution (Ijirigho, 2009). Users anticipate from the academic libraries the accompanying viewpoints; completeness, openness, quick satisfaction, takes after capacity of data, usability and different organizations and media (Nyamache et al, 2012).

Payne and Waller (2000) express this perspective by saying: despite these difficulties, libraries are progressively taking a gender at better approaches for giving help and support services, including the expanded utilization of instructional toward oneself materials, virtual help and phone/email services (Ijirigho, 2010). Development in internet usage, a proceeding with expansion and accessibility of electronic resources and changes to the delivery of information keep on having an enormous effect on libraries and the expectations of our users. There are both likenesses and contrasts in the procurement of reference and the delivery of information to on location and offsite users. With the appearance of the digital library and a shifting information panorama, conventional library exercises are experiencing challenge and transform and none more so than the administration and delivery of reference services.

In the past a library's collection was what it physically possessed and housed and resources were recorded in the Library's catalogue. Today libraries give access to an incomprehensible cluster of information resources some of which it possesses, its physical collection, yet quite a bit of it authorized access to remote electronic collections, databases, electronic journals or e-Books, digital pictures or a wide variety of links to free sites. In several libraries not all resources are open through the catalogue and users should regularly explore different parts of a library's website in a pursuit for resources to successfully meet their information needs. Many users might never completely investigate the boundless scope of resources accessible to them because of the difficulties postured by resources discovery.

Present and future library services must be user oriented. Library management must get back feedbacks from users and consider the appraisal of services as a critical viewpoint for creating right objectives and strategies. Library ought not to work altogether disengagement from its users' expectations. Libraries leaders must know the users' expectations to enhance the nature of services offered (Scott, 1992).

CHANGING STUDENTS EXPECTATIONS

It is clear to all who work in Technical Education that student desires have changed throughout the most recent three decades. Technical institutes now end up being pushed from one perspective to respond to mounting students desires, while on the other there are reasons for alarm that the major motivation behind Technical Education could be bended or even lost if institutions go too far toward setting Technical Education on a business grip.

Students' expectations are now high and as Davies (2002) focuses out, these now include:

- Flexibility and decision in the delivery of education;
- Access to front line innovation;
- A two way correspondence prepare in the middle of themselves and with the university/institution
- To be counseled about the learning experience;
- Accurate information about their courses, evaluation methodology, affirmations process, and so on and
- Honesty as for whether their needs can be met or not

To these we might likewise include:

- Quality and polished skill in the procurement of administrations
- Access to suitably qualified teachers and suitable learning support
- Value of study to prospects

RESPONDING TO USERS EXPECTATIONS AND CHANGING NEEDS

Technical institution libraries are quite advanced and using lot of web based services for their users and trying to fulfill their expectations and changing needs. In this regard some important steps have been taken as follows:

- IIT and other engineering and business management libraries have made a commitment for open access publishing.
- Users have increasing expectations for online content. Mostly science and technology users expect online contents, and humanities users are still desire ready access to print materials. The changes in user expectations will keep on challenging libraries as well.
- Awareness programs have been conducted to educate faculty on scholarly communication issues and provide assistance to faculty in publishing their research output.
- The increase in electronic resources sets an increased demand on the network infrastructure and on staff to negotiate licenses, design more intuitive web interfaces, and assist users in accessing library resources.

- IIT , NIT, IIM libraries are providing support for emerging forms of content, such as blogs, podcasts, and wikis and consider the implications of new devices for viewing content.
- The IIT Libraries have made a strategy for supporting a digital reference collection and promoting its usage.
- These Libraries are using optimal methods for collection analysis and assessment.
- By partnering with larger institutions in the state, higher Technical institutions like IIT, NIT, IIIT, NISER and IISERare able to subscribe to packages of journals and databases that would otherwise be high-priced. It is important to sustain in up to date collections through cooperative licenses and look for future opportunities. All these institutions are members of INDEST consortium.
- Remembering the end goal to meet effectively meet the unique programming and dataset needs of the higher research and technical institutes, designated funding are being allocated on a continuing basis with periodic adjustments for price increases and licensing changes.
- Preservation of digital content is major concern of every library including purchased content and unique content held in special collections.

SERVICES

Students like to utilize virtual services and spaces for discovering information. They additionally need effortlessly safe systems that depict clear ways to information. Engineering and other higher technical institution libraries must utilize the information of users' inclination for services like Google and Yahoo to make instinctive pursuit ways and steady pages that give purpose of-need support.

Use of the library's virtual resources keeps on expanding. Staffing and upkeep of the virtual services must be enough tended to.

The library system confronts a few difficulties like bringing together library communication, fund development and coordinating academic departments. Librarians expressed a requirement for more coordination in this system with a specific end goal to investigate how to best serve their users.

With upgrades in database technology and searching techniques, the usefulness of the integrated library system (ILS) as a revelation apparatus must make strides.

The multifaceted nature of library instruction rivals the shortage of time every contact link has with users.

The library will expand endeavors to team up with faculty on forming information proficiency assignments into major coursework.

Reference as a service must serve as becoming non-conventional users' populace. Have user desires and practices changed, as well as the information they have to get to change likewise. The effortlessness of the generally defined library reference service misrepresents its unpredicted.

CHANGES IN LIBRARIES

Some key challenges and changes faced by the libraries today are :

- Decreasing footfalls
- Internet vs. print media
- Catering to the SMS generation whose tolerance level is low
- Card catalogues have gone down
- Reference collections are not upgraded and very less utilized by users
- Now users are not willing to visit the library to study and utilize the print resources
- Photocopying services have been decreased because of availability of e-resources subsequently the users are utilizing their portable camera, smart phone and tablet etc.
- Library staff aided circulation system supplanted with RFID empower circulation system
- Microfilms and Microfiches have not utilized/services and hence have been shut down.

- Accessibility of e-journals back volumes of journals is very less in use.
- Back volumes of abstracting and indexing journals are not used by users.
- 70-80% of library budget are spending for subscription of e-resources.
- Due to accessibility of e-resources, numerous sections have been closed.
- Now many libraries have started online payment system for procurement of books and library over dues through debit/credit card
- Libraries are permitting users to bring their Laptop inside the library for study as opposed to reading books.
- Libraries are giving more electric amenities and Wi-Fi access points in the Library for portable computer connection and Internet access.
- Libraries are giving open to perusing zone (lights, funs, tables, seats, A/C, and so forth.
- Libraries are introducing CCTV surveillance system for library resources.
- Due to space problem a large portion of the academic libraries are subscribing e-resources rather than print based collection aside from course books.
- All New IITs, IISERs and different Institutions are subscribing lot of e-resources, (current and back issues), eBooks and e-databases in electronic form because of space problems and due to lack of library staff. They are obtaining just reading material in print structure.
- The University Grant Commission (UGC) has decided to give costly e-journals free of cost to the research scholars from 12th plan beginning from April 2012.
- Users are collecting their resources from different sources in India and abroad through email and imparting one another.
- Libraries are running under staff because of retirement and moreover no new recruitments are made.

- Institutional authorities are not persuading to recruit new library staff because of availability of online resources and services.

Several changes have taken place in the sphere of Technical institution libraries. The factors creating these changes may be categorized as economics, technology, higher education and human resource. As one of the key players in data world, IIT libraries have immediate impact of the progressions. Economic factor is the most prominent component which is affecting the library activities in numerous ways. The best concern is that the library trusts are reducing while the expenses of all library materials have risen. Coupled with this, is the expanded interest for books and journals both in print and electronic form. This shrinking or stagnant subsidizing has prompted utilization of management strategies to build effectiveness. This has additionally made the libraries to search for alternative resources by charging certain services or marketing of information.

Over the past few years, there has been an increase of machine applications for library and information work. This has brought tremendous changes in the role of libraries. Libraries have exploited the new information technologies to provide an extensive variety of services and products, which were unrealistic, a few decades ago. Today CD-ROMs and online search services have revolutionized the provision of services to the users. Without information technology libraries would have never possessed the capacity to fulfill the changing needs of users in an informative era of today. In the recent times the issue has is of great concern because of multidisciplinary approaches to research. IIT libraries have been on the cutting edge of computerization in India. They have effectively modernized their libraries utilizing the most recent information technology (Singh, 2001).

LIBRARY ACTIVITIES AND USERS EXPECTATIONS

Libraries have been compelled to meet the rising expectations of the users in an era of shrinking budgets. Technology factor has introduced and exactness in numerous spheres of library activities like making choices for systems administration to give access to limitless store of electronic information and for automation of various housekeeping operations, yet this has likewise added to the weight of tight library resources, as funds need to channelized for buy of equipment and infrastructure for IT based services. Other than this, the library managers need to adapt up to outdated nature and similarity of hardware and software which includes lot of investment. The sheer amount of information accessible electronically is itself a challenge to the library proficient. A percentage of the users are profoundly techno savvy, consequently all the more requesting furthermore now and again disappointed with the level of service they get. The paradox of modern libraries are that the user's computer proficiency ranges from least to the most elevated amount and the staff needs to make available services to all the categories of users. Subsequently the preparation of the staff for effective utilization of IT services is extremely significant.

In spite of the fact that it is expensive yet this must be carried out as a regular procedure. Technical education has experienced plentiful changes and generally has picked up a great deal of magnitude under Knowledge Commission. The eventual fate of academic libraries will be controlled by their capacity to adjust to their changing surroundings and to deal with the change successfully.

Libraries associated to organizations of higher learning need to indulge shifted needs of user groups which is a heterogeneous mixture of part time student, distance learners, research students, teachers and scientists and the library services need to range from most fundamental needs of a few users to profoundly particular needs of researchers and scientists. In the event that all the over three elements clear path for the changes in the libraries, it is the fourth element, i.e. the human resources which needs to usher these changes. Any change or advancement is conceivable just in a favourable organizational environment. This is conceivable by human resources improvement in the organization as change can just live in an inventive imperative work environment. By understanding and responding to individuals, their reasons for alarm and needs, the change procedure can be facilitated and right organization environment can be made.

TRENDS IN THE TECHNICAL LIBRARIES

The utilization patterns of users are marked as follows:

- Demand for print materials from the stacks is diminishing
- Usage of electronic resources is expanding (Wilson &Triffett, 2009)
- Traditional eye to eye reference is declining more individuals seem, by all accounts, to be discovering what they require through e-resources accessible on the PCs in the Reading rooms or through search engines on the web. Utilization of the phone service is changing and interest is dropping.
- Demand for electronic reference services is expanding with the increase in the number quantities of fax machines and the practice of writing letters is declining.
- Website utilization is increasing

There are various factors responsible to bring changes in library management with specific reference to Indian technical libraries; some of them are listed below:

- E-learning
- Open Archives
- Library Consortia
- Metadata Standards
- Changing Users Expectations
- Resource Sharing
- Industrial Interaction
- Quality Based Library and Information Services
- Need Based User Education
- Digital Library Initiatives
- Recent Trends and Developments
- Resource Crunch

CONCLUSION

Technical libraries cannot prepare effectively for the future or position themselves on grounds until they understand their changing roles in the current learning and research environment, which is drastically unique in relation to the environment a decade ago. Understanding and assessing library users changing information needs and to provide the service as per their expectation is a challenging task for these libraries.

The development and delivery of high-quality users service is an important goal for any libraries in technical education. The libraries are changing from storehouse of books to dynamic service center. . It can be concluded that the engineering and other technical institutions libraries need to provide web-based library and information services to the users under intranet and Internet environment. It is also noted that there is great desire among the users to implement the library and information service through Institute website. There is also a need to plan an integrated training programme for the users as well as the library staff for an effective utilization of services. A regular feedback from the faculty and students will also go a long way in improving the library services and their changing expectations can be met effectively.

REFERENCES

1. Babu, R. B., Vinayagamoorthy, P. & Gopalakrishnan, S. (2007). ICT skills among librarians in engineering educational institutions in Tamil Nadu. DESIDOC Bulletin of Information Technology, 27(6), 55-64.
2. Bawden, D. &Vilar, P. (2006). Digital Libraries: to meet or manage user expectations. ASLIB Proceedings, 58(4), 346-354 (*www.emraldinsight.com*)
3. Harish Chandra (2004). Capacity Building in Technical Libraries., In National Smposium on Capacity Building in Technical Libraries in the Present Digital Era, Chennai (India), 5-6 Nov, 2004. [Conference paper]. eprints.rclis.org/6582/1/Capacity_Building.doc
4. Jayasundara, C. C. (2008). User Perceptions and Expectations on E-Information Literacy Development Programmes. National University Library, 10(4), 82.
5. Jayasuriya, H. K. & Brillantine, F. (2007). Student services in the 21st century: evolution and innovation in discovering student needs, teaching information literacy,

and designing Library 2.0 based services. Legal Reference Services Quarterly, 26(1), 135-70.

6. Jotwani, D. (2014). Marketing of Electronic Resources in IIT Libraries.DESIDOC Journal of Library & Information Technology, 34(2), 162-169.
7. Kenneth, R. Teas (1993). Expectations, Performance Evaluation, and Customers' Perceptions of Quality. Journal of Marketing, 57,(4), 18-34.
8. MacColl, John. (1999). User expectations of the hybrid library. The New Review of Information and Library Research, 5, 121-131.
9. Sadeh, T. (2007). Time for a change: new approaches for a new generation of library users. New Library World, 108(7/8), 307-316, available at: *http://www.emeraldinsight.com/10.1108/03074800710763608*
10. Sampath Kumar, P. T. & Kumar, G. T. (2010). Perceptions and usage of eresources and internet by Indian academics. The Electronic Library, 28(1), 137-156.
11. Tam, L.W.H. & Robertson, A. C. (2002). Managing change: libraries and information services in the digital age. Library Management, 23(8), 369-377. Available at: http://unllib.unl.edu/LPP/shahid.htm.
12. Xia, W. (2003). Digital library services: perceptions and expectations of user communities and librarians in a New Zealand academic library. Australian Academic and Research Libraries, 34(1), 56-70, available at: http://alia.org.au/publishing/aarl/34.1/full. text/xia.htm (accessed 6 April 2006).

12

Role of Leadership in Library and Information Centres in Digital Environment

Brundaban Nahak*

ABSTRACT

The Librarianship a noble profession conceived earlier and now has transformed tremendously with regards to collections, technology, staff, finance, users and services. Leadership is one of the specialized area being emphasized today as one of the key competency for librarians managing the academic and research libraries for better productivity, visibility and development of functional and innovative libraries. Unlike the countries like USA and UK, the concept of library leadership is gradually occupying significance in India and as such attempts have been made to explore the significance and growth of library leadership in Indian context and literature generated over a period of time on leadership in library and information science. Effective communication channels need to be in place so library staffs are informed and aware of recent developments. The library managers themselves also have to be prepared to take on visions that they may not have

* Librarian, Radha Krushna Institute of Technology and Engineering (RITE), Bhubaneswar, Odisha

originated. Mutual trust has to be present between managers and other library staff. There is tension for the library manager in having a background profile whilst at the same time being highly sensitive and aware to what is currently happening. The major challenge for the library manager is the actions they need to take when trust or communication or intrinsic motivation etc is not present in the library. This article describes the definition, theory, characteristics, types, literature review, competence, ethics and development of leadership in library. This article also explores the leadership activities, implication, attributes, issues of leadership, etc.It is an attempt to touch base with all the areas relating to leadership in library and information centers simple languages. The leadership plays an important role in the library and information centers now days.

Keywords : Leadership; Library Management; Competencies.

INTRODUCTION

Leadership is essentially a subject of management research. It is however a theme that is relevant to all human endeavors. Business enterprises and corporations have embraced the application of leadership principles and have found them to be agents of productivity and profitability. The time is therefore ripe for the Library and Information Professionals, particularly in this part of the world, to take a cue from the latter's experiences to enhance professionalism, information service delivery as well as social/educational relevance of practitioners. The leadership qualities of a person create a niche for him and a combination of leadership competencies of managers in the workplace brings corporate success. "Leadership is about listening to people, supporting and encouraging them and involving them in the decision-making and problem-solving processing. It is about building teams and developing their ability to make skilful decisions" - (Stuart Levine and Michael Crom, 1994).

Library Leadership refers to the ability of a Librarian or head of the library to lead the team of subordinate library professionals and supporting staff with utmost confidence and diligence by his/ her act of benevolence showing passion for creativity, innovation and development of library on par excellence creating congenial atmosphere and subordinate staff should also feel and execute duties and responsibilities to achieve the mission of the library moving in the same direction as of library leader. In the words of Boer, Bothma and Olwagen (2012) library leadership as "The ability to be visionary, to embrace change and to anticipate future information technologies, thereby providing strategic direction for their libraries and the ability to motivate their colleagues to share the vision, will empower library leaders for the digital demands of the 21st century". Leadership has to take place every day. It cannot be the responsibility of the few , a rare event or a once-in-a-lifetime opportunity. The library and information organizations are exception in their need for good leadership to ensure good management as well as attainment of organizational objectives. One may wish to add that the subject of Leadership has been neglected in the library and information profession until the 1980s. The ageing process itself makes the education and development of future leaders very expedient.

The ideas around leadership for all in libraries will then be described within the context of the wider perspectives. In terms of achieving leadership for all in libraries, the following strategies will be considered: sharing the vision, trust, action learning and managing communication Librarians are a group of highly skilled, educated, and motivated professionals, and leadership with a light hand is the best way to take full advantage of their expertise. Leadership is not magnetic personality that can just as well be a glib tongue. It is not 'making friends and influencing people,' that is flattery. Leadership is lifting a person's vision to higher sights, the raising of a person's performance to a higher standard, the building of a personality beyond its normal limitations. The leadership plays an important role in the library and information centers now days.

DEFINITION OF LEADERSHIP

There is no single, universal accepted definition of a leadership. At a broad level, the common characteristic of a leadership is that he should be ahead of others and have the ability to attribute his thoughts clearly. Many authors have defined the term leadership and some of the important definitions are given as :

The process of social influence in which one person can enlist the aid and support of other in the accomplishment of a common task.(Chemmers, 2002 as cited in Wikipedia 2009).

Wikipedia (2009) further cited a people driven definition of Keith 2007 as Leadership is ultimately creating a way for people to contribute to making something extraordinary happen.

Leadership is the relation function between an individual and a group around some common interest and behaving in a manner directed or determined by them.(Encyclopedia of Social Science).

Leadership is "the ability of influencing people to strive willing for mutual objective". — **Terry**

Chemmers (2002), another source submitted as Leadership is a process by which a person influences others to accomplish an objective and direct the organization in a way that makes it cohesive and coherent. Leaders carry out this process by applying their Leadership attributes, such as beliefs, values, ethics, character, knowledge, and skills. (Concepts of Leadership (1997).

Covey (2004) opined that Leadership is creating an environment in which people want to be part of the organization and not just work for the organization. Leadership creates an environment that makes people, want to, "rather than have to" do.

Tao Te Ching (66:6-7, New English Version) As an ancient philosopher once said, "If you want to lead the people, you must learn how to follow them".

Library Leadership is a part of Library Management, but today the concept of leadership has become more of inter-disciplinary nature and is growing as a specialized subject. The term 'Leadership qualities or Leader' is normally a mouth word of the society when there is an achievement either in the political system or higher education or any other system providing credit to the personality acknowledging his/ her leadership quality or vision or being a good leader.

Stuart Levine and Michael Crom (1994). Leadership is about listening to people, supporting and encouraging them and involving them in the decision-making and problem-solving processing. It is about building teams and developing their ability to make skilful decisions.

LITERATURE REVIEW

Leadership is a topic that has garnered much scholarly attention in the general management and social sciences literature, leadership in the context of library administration has only recently become an area of interest in the library science literature. It is found from the existing primary and secondary sources that, the literature on "Leadership" in library and information science is a new and unexplored area in the context of Indian librarianship, but a considerable body of research literature on traits and competencies of library leaders are found at international level. Most of the literature is in the form of articles or conference papers.

Needham (2001) stresses several important leadership roles to play in creating an environment to nurture a successful transition of libraries into the new roles they will play. Among these roles are helping to create standards and protocols, advocacy, mentoring, creating heroes, and underwriting leadership training for new members of the profession.

Winston and Dunkley (2002) re-conceptualized the importance of the competencies that librarian leaders will need in the future. Probably Library leadership is not much heard especially in the Indian context unlike in USA or UK librarianship.

Arora (2004) highlighted leadership skills and personal traits that were used successfully for transforming a traditional library into a hybrid library in precarious circumstances and conditions that exist in some of the organizations in India. It describes the management techniques, skills and personal traits of a leader that were used to motivate staff members to computerize the library, to improve library services and to transform a traditional library into a hybrid library.

Boer, Bothma and Olwagen (2012) library leadership as

"the ability to be visionary, to embrace change and to anticipate future information technologies, thereby providing strategic direction for their libraries and the ability to motivate their colleagues to share the vision, will empower library leaders for the digital demands of the 21st century".

Jordan, Mary Wilkins (2011) has provided a list of skills required for an effective leadership are:

Table 1. Leadership versus Management as proposed by Mason & Wetherbee (2004) and adopted by Wang and Su (2004).

• Vision	• Creativity
• Flexibility	• Self-awareness
• Communication skills	• Ambition
• Teamwork	• Previousexperience
• Interpersonal skills	• Conflict resolution
• Employee centered	• Tenacity
• Risk taking	• Planning
• Customer service	• Personal energy
• Multicultural awareness	• Accountability
• Problem solving	• Delegation
• Motivating others	• Self-confidence
• Commitment to the profession	• Emotional intelligence
• Integrity	• Mentoring
• Enthusiasm	• Demonstrating leadership
• Modeling values	• Resource management
• Intelligence and	• Time management
• Diplomacy	• Sense of humor
	• Credibility

Table 2. Leadership versus Management (Wikipedia 2009)

Leadership	Management
A leader does the right things.	A good manager does things right.
Leadership is about effectiveness.	Management is largely about efficiency.
Leading is about what and why.	Management is about how to do things.

Leadership is about trust and about people.	Management is about Systems, controls, procedures, policies, and structure
Leadership is about innovating and initiating.	Management is about copying, about managing the status quo.
Leadership looks at the horizon not just the bottom line.	Management is about the bottom line.

Leadership	**Management**
Leaders innovate.	Managers administer.
Leaders ask what and why.	Managers ask how and when.
Leaders focus on people.	Managers focus on systems.
Leaders do the right things.	Managers do things right.
Leaders develop.	Managers maintain.
Leaders inspire trust.	Managers rely on control.
Leaders have long term perspective.	Managers have short-term perspective.
Leaders challenge the status quo.	Managers accept the status quo.
Leaders have an eye on the horizon.	Managers have an eye on the bottom-line.
Leaders originate.	Managers imitate.
Leaders are their own persons.	Managers emulate the classic good soldier.
Leaders show originality.	Managers copy.

TYPES OF LEADERS

Closely related to theories of leadership is the issue of leadership typology. The following have been identified as variation in leadership styles as enumerated in Concepts of leadership (1997):

Authoritarian Leader : (high task, low relationship) : This category of leaders are task-oriented (i.e. workaholic) but are very hard on their workers. There is no room for collaboration and the leaders want to remain unquestionable.

Team Leader : (high task, high relationship) : This type of leader serves as a role model as he leads by positive example. Team spirit is encouraged and potentialities of members are developed.

Country Club Leader : (Low task, high relationship) : The type of leader takes advantage of people as he hangs on the use of rewards to secure cooperation and maintain discipline.

Impoverished Leader : (Low task, low relationship) : This has been aptly described as a leader who uses a "delegate and disappear" management style. There is generally lack of commitment and accomplishment is also absent.

Leadership Skills and Competencies : Literature has presented diverse approach to the subject of leadership skills. However, Nye (2004) has succinctly categorized leadership skills into four, although in relation to librarianship, but adopted from general leadership principles as thus:

Organization : This includes the ability to organize people, projects, and meeting agenda.

Communication : Ability to communicate well is very germane to fruitful relationship and success of a leader. Giving relevant and timely information as well as the expectation of feedbacks from stakeholders are desirable.

Hopefulness : The leader requires a high degree of optimism to forge through difficult times. He must always give the assurance of a positive outcome.

Praise & Celebration : Individual and group contributions and successes need to be acknowledged. The celebration of such gives further encouragement to those involved.

However, Concepts of Leadership (1997) further articulated eleven Principles.

LEADERSHIP COMPETENCIES

There is difference between a leader and a manager, as well as competence and competencies. A leader facilitates change but a manager maintains the status quo. Similarly, competence means mastery and competencies mean a set of skills. Competence comes with experience. But before that we must have a good commonsense and formal education. Then strategic professional learning must be internalized by the LIPs as a lifelong learning process. LIPs must be equipped with cultural literacy and information skills for learning. Similarly, a sense of responsibility and accountability along with team spirit, motivation, and interpersonal skills should also become a part of their mind, body, and soul.

LIBRARY LEADERSHIP: MODELS AND COMPETENCIES

"Leadership is about listening to people, supporting and encouraging them and involving them in the decision-making and problem-solving processing. It is about building teams and developing their ability to make skilful decisions" - (Stuart Levine and Michael Crom, 1994).Library Leadership refers to the ability of a Librarian or head of the library to lead the team of subordinate library professionals and supporting staff with utmost confidence and diligence by his/ her act of benevolence showing passion for creativity, innovation and development of library on par excellence creating congenial atmosphere and subordinate staff should also feel and execute duties and responsibilities to achieve the mission of the library moving in the same direction as of library leader. In the words of Boer, Bothma and Olwagen (2012) library leadership as "The ability to be visionary, to embrace change and to anticipate future information technologies, thereby providing strategic direction for their libraries and the ability to motivate their colleagues to share the vision, will empower library leaders for the digital demands of the 21st century".The Competencies of Successful Leader emphasized by various stalwarts in library profession and are made to know the various leadership models for the benefit of librarians to understand, measure and evaluate the strength of leadership and strive to possess the competencies

LEADERSHIP CHARACTERISTICS

As illustrated in Competent Leader-ship: What Effective Leaders Do Well, some common characteristics and behaviors of effective leaders are as follows:

- Efficient coaching skills, Confidence, Consistency between word and action – "walking the talk"
- Creativity, Empathic listening skills, self confidence
- Being visionary, Inspiring, Long-term focus
- Maintaining a balance, between individual needs and team needs

- Awareness of realistic , conditions, Strong self-esteem
- Sense of priorities, Service mentality, Sincerity
- Technical or contextual, expertise, Trust
- Willingness to share, responsibility
- Willingness to share &credit or recognition

ISSUES IN THE LEADERSHIP IN LIS PROFESSIONS

Despite all the theoretical bases for leadership, the leadership role of a leader cannot be divulged from his basic functions in a specific situation. The highlights of some issues of leadership in LIS professions are given as thus:

- Leadership is just one dimension of the managers work
- It involves "the exercise of social influence by infusing the parent organization with purpose and direction in order to achieve its goals.
- Leadership requires that the library director should influence members of the parent institutions to provide resources in order t (a) support expansion plans (b) accept the goals of the library as valid and deserving support.
- The 3 dimensions used to measure library leadership are (a) Leader activities (b) Management of organizational change (c) Reputational Effectiveness.
- Leader Activities and Managerial role activities
- Professional activities and involvement
- Membership on community committees
- Strategies for influencing the environment.
- One of the most obvious explanations of the failure of leadership in our time is that so few of our leaders-and our potential leaders –seem to have any road map. It is hard to lead when you yourself are in a labyrinth.

LEADERSHIP THEORIES

This paper has adopted the format of presentation of the eight universally accepted theories of leadership as cited in Wang, & Suns (2006) work.

Table 3. Leaderships Theory and Assumptions (Wang & Su (2006)

Types	Assumptions
Great Man Theory	• Leaders are born and not made • Great leaders will arise when there is a great need.
Trait Theory	• People are born with inherited traits. • Some traits are particularly suited for leadership. • People who make good leaders have the right (or sufficient) combination of traits
Behavioral Theory	• Leaders can be made, rather than are born. • Successful leadership is based on definable, learned behaviour.
Participative Leadership	• Involvement in decision making improves the understanding of the issues involved by those who must carry out the decisions. • People are more committed to actions where they have [sic] involved in the relevant decision-making. • People are less competitive and are more collaborative when they are working on joint goals. When people make decisions together, the social commitment to one another is greater and thus increase their commitment to the decision.
Situational Leadership	• The best action of the leader depends on a range of situational factors.
Contingency Theory	• The leaders ability to lead is contingent upon various situational factors, including the leader's preferred style, the capabilities and behaviours of followers and also various other situational factors.
Transactional Leadership	• People are motivated by reward and punishment.

- Social systems work best with a clear chain of command.
- When people have agreed to do a job. a pan of the deal is that they cede all authority to their manager.
- The prime purpose of a subordinate is to do what their manager tells them to do.
- People will follow a person who inspires them.
- A person with vision and passion can achieve great things.
- The way to get things done is by injecting enthusiasm and energy

SIX MANAGERIAL ROLE/ACTIVITIES FOE LIBRARIAN AS LEADER

Supervisor Role : which involves directing the work of subordinates; integrating subordinates goals with the library's goals and objectives; allocating human resources to tasks; evaluating subordinates job performance; resolving conflicts between subordinates and providing new staff with training.

Liaison Role : Involves attending social functions for contacts; attendance at conferences/meetings; maintaining informal communication networks; and relating with people outside.

Environment Monitor Role : Includes initiating new ideas for services and operations; keeping up with professional trends/ changes; keeping abreast of technological developments; scanning the environment for new opportunities to improve services/operations; collecting information about users touring facilities to observe and reading reports of other units.

Entrepreneur Role : Involves planning and implementing changes in the library, initiating change in the library and solving problems by instituting changes in the library.

Spokesman Role : Includes serving as an expert or advising people outside the library; keeping others abreast of developments in the library, attending to correspondences, and serving on committees, and representing the library.

Management of Organizational Change : Changes in organizational domain vis a vis other community/cognate entities; Internal changes

THE LIBRARY/ INFORMATION SCIENCE PROFESSIONALS LEADERSHIP AGENDA/STRATEGIES

The following initiatives are desirable and could be found rewarding:

- Creation of awareness for need of leadership development skills among professionals.
- Self development in leadership skills by Librarians and Information Professionals.
- Integration of leadership development into the library/ information centre strategic planning.
- Leadership Development Programme to run through the ladder (i.e. from the top to bottom).
- Library and Information Schools to integrate Leadership Skills development into their curricula.
- Need for librarians and information professionals to maintain strong network within and without their organization to enhance development of skills and knowledge.

IMPLICATIONS OF LEADERSHIP FOR ALL FOR LIBRARY MANAGEMENT

Very little has been written in the library management literature which explicitly advocates that leadership skills are generic and should be present in all staff. There is an acknowledgment by Stephens and Russell that there is pressure to look at this approach. When reviewing the recent ideas about leadership they found a focus on leadership development in all employees. Their support was less than fulsome when they advocated that 'libraries should broaden their efforts to embrace experiments in the use of these newer approaches to leadership'. The library manager has to focus more on giving employees the flexibility to adapt to an environment where there is constant change. This departure from command and control is directing library managers to become the facilitative leader. The leader who can take the role of a facilitator blends his or her role of visionary decisive leader with that of listening and empowering leader. As a facilitative leader heor she involves followers as much as possible in creating the group's vision and purpose, carrying out the vision and purpose and building a productive and cohesive team. Facilitation skills are becoming recognized as part of the repertoire of the new library managers. The leadership fits well into libraries because it is compatible with other tools and principles in libraries. The mangers role is to create the facilitative environment in the library where individuals at every level can:

- have some individuality of thought and actions
- set some standards to monitor their own performance
- be able to interpret events without fear of making mistakes
- respond to events without having to follow the rulebook all the time

There are barriers to effective leadership for all in libraries. There are some library staff who would like top-down, directive leadership as they just like to be told what to do. Over the years, most libraries have developed very powerful hierarchies and also rigid traditions which do not allow the concept of leadership for all to flourish. If the hierarchy is very influential, there will be little room for development and creativity. The hierarchy forces people to create boundaries around their different needs and relationships. If this culture does not change, employees will not think creatively or relish risk taking. Neither will they show enthusiasm or passion about their work and library.

PERSONAL ATTRIBUTES

(a) Principled / Ethical

- Practices principles above personalities
- Stands up for what he/she believes in
- Makes decisions without begin swayed by political expediency
- Considers the ethical implications of all personal actions and organizational activity

(b) Honest

- Conducts conversations with others in a professional manner
- Addresses all issues—even sensitive issues—as they arise

(c) Humble

- Gives credit to others as well as one's self when a task is completed
- Admits limitations and mistakes

(d) Gracious

- Maintains a positive attitude in critical situations
- Mitigates gossip and other negative influences in the workplace
- Open and professional with others despite personal feelings
- Acknowledges when another does something positive or helpful for the institution

(e) Teachable

- Identifies when assistance is needed and willing to ask for help
- Internalizes lessons learned from experiences for future use
- Accepts questions and input from others
- Influenced, but not manipulated, by others

Five categories of personal attributes emerged: principled/ ethical, honest, humble, gracious, and teachable

DEVELOPING LEADERSHIP FOR ALL IN THE LIBRARY

Leadership for all as a principle will not develop organically in a library. There has to bevarious explicit commitments and strategies to allow it to flourish. Included in these are:

Sharing the vision : the importance of the shared vision has already been alluded to the library manager supports the library staff develop a single vision together. The library manager has to be patient as the vision is identified, developed and refined. The manager tries to ensure there is consistency between their own vision and that of the rest of the library staff.

Trust : unless the manager trusts the library employee, leadership for all will never materialize. Libraries have traditionally found it difficult to allow their staff to be able to interpret events themselves and have individuality of thought and practice. After years of telling people what to do, library managers have to have a belief that their employees are responsible and committed.

Action learning : when considering leadership for all, having action learning in place is seen as a very effective way to support its development. In terms of leadership development, action learning allows competencies such as 'adaptive thinking ,building relations, inspiring trust, aligning the organization, fostering open and effective communication, demonstrating vision and focusing on quality and continuous improvement. For a library, a major strength of action learning is that it does not require any special set of conditions; it works just as well in a bureaucracy as it does in a flat organization.

Making communication work : libraries and organizations, which are employing social animals (staff) that ensure the service is delivered. As social animals, interaction and communication takes place all the time in formal or informal meetings. These meetings are very important within the context of leadership for all. The library manager has to therefore ensure employees have enhanced interpersonal and communication skills. If they understand each other more and are comfortable in opening up to their colleagues, the underpinning leadership for all should emerge. The library staffs have well developed interpersonal communication skills among themselves the library service will be excellent.

QUALITIES OF A LEADER

A leader has certain inherent qualities and traits, which assists him, in directing and guiding role to influence the people. Some of these traits according to Stogdill are as given below:

- Physical features

- Intelligence
- Social skills
- Emotional stability
- Human relations
- Empathy
- Objectivity
- Motivating skills
- Technical skills
- Communication skills

LIBRARY ADVOCACY

Library leaders are increasingly being asked to promote their libraries and explain their value as a public good to the general public and government leaders, in order to ensure their own sustainability. Experts overwhelmingly identified a critical need for librarians to understand and lead advocacy efforts on behalf of their libraries, but less than two-thirds of programs teach librarians how to do so. To address this gap, ad-hoc workshops and programming have been developed to provide librarians with training on advocacy skills. However, these workshops offer a less-comprehensive perspective than leadership-training programs with a focus on advocacy.

INDIAN STUDIES ON LEADERSHIP

The Information Society has brought about developments in the way information is created, consolidated and accessed. ICT has produced larger volumes of information, new ways of packaging information and new tools for managing information. These developments require leadership skills of librarians and other information workers to meet the demands of the global economy for information resources and services. The rapid developments in computer technology as well as economic changes have made it clear that the familiar role of the 21st Century Librarian as information intermediaries must undergo immense change, if Librarians are to avoid being displaced by a variety of content providers.

Krishan Gopal (2006) The societal, organizational, and

competitive changes affecting academic libraries point to the need for effective leadership and the identification of an important component of such a statement of leadership competencies.

Prakash and Patil(2011) discussed the leadership skills in the changing management perspectives of libraries and information centres.

Jagtap and Kapade (2011) highlighted the values of leadership in academic and research libraries.

Jange and Sujatha (2011) explored the challenges faced by library professionals in managing the libraries, technological skills required and leadership qualities needed for present and future Library Professionals to effectively render need based information services to the user community.

Ramesh Babu (2012)Leadership skills for professional competencies, management, networking and teamwork are the need of the hour.

Jange (2012) attempted to identify and explore the significance of Leadership roles among Library and Information Science professionals that can be leveraged as a strategic asset to attract staff, create favorable assessments.

ETHICS IN LEADERSHIP

Leadership requires courage, good communication skills and the ability to resolve ethical dilemmas. Determining what is right or ethical is one of the most difficult skills an individual must develop. But make no mistake, doing what is "right" is a requirement of effective leadership." Ethic is a part of the organizational climate. Top managers serve as leaders within their organization. Ethic can be defined as the set of principles and values that govern the behaviors of an individual or a group with respect to what is right and what is wrong.

CONCLUSION

Library leadership is the need of the hour but this is still a very primitive stage in Indian academic librarianship, which is more heard than practiced. This calls for specialized training for library managers for their better productivity and performance.

It is our normal practice to acknowledge in terms of his/ her leadership, when librarians outclass development or performance of library on par excellence. Library leadership though part of curriculum of 'Library management' but is not a specialized area. Unfortunately, especially in the state university setup, most of the libraries lack appointment of University librarian and is mainly managed by Dy.Librarian or Assistant Librarians. In Odisha state, out of 16 state universities, only four universities has full time librarian. The question of leadership becomes secondary to some extent, as it requires a full fledge librarian. It is said that leaders are born not created. But what so ever, the reason as to why lot of hue and cry of leadership is for better productivity, visibility and strengthening of libraries and this can be achieved only with the strong leadership of head librarian who shows, excels and leads the team with utmost diligence and act of benevolence to meet the customer expectations. The challenge for the library manager is to have the courage, the belief and the trust to take the principles of leadership for all and apply them to their own library. If leader is good then the library can run better and smoothly with better rending library services with the help of library staff.

REFERENCE

1. Ammons-Stephens, Shorlette; Cole, Holly J.; Jenkins-Gibbs, Keisha; Riehle, Catherine Fraser; and Weare, William H. Jr.(2009). Developing Core Leadership Competencies for the Library Profession.. Libraries Faculty and Staff Scholarship and Research. Paper 19. *http://docs.lib.purdue.edu/lib_fsdocs/*
2. Ansari, Husain al and Khadher, Othman al (2011). Developing a Leadership Competency Model for Library and Information Professionals in Kuwait. Libri, Vol. 61, pp. 239–246.
3. Arora, Jagdish (2004). Transforming a Traditional Library into a Hybrid Library: Use of Leadership and Managerial Skills at the Central Library, IIT Delhi, Science & Technology Libraries, 23(2-3): 5-15.
4. Boer, Ann-Louise de', Bothma, J D and Olwagen, Johan (2012). Library leadership: Innovative options for designing training programmes to build leadership competencies in the digital age. SAJnl Ubs & Info Sei 2012, 78(2)

5. Chemmers, M. M. (2002). Cognitive, Social and emotional intelligence of transformational leadership: efficacy and effectiveness. In multiple intelligence Riggio S. E. and Murphy F. J. (eds.).

6. Christopher Soo-Guan Khoo (2005). Competencies for New Era Librarians and Information Professionals, ICOL 2005 conference. Concepts of leadership (1997) created May 11, 1997; updated May 21, 2008. Retrieved October 6, 2009 from *http:// www.nwlink.com/odonclark/leader/leadcon.html.*

7. Covey, Stephen R. (2004). The 8th habit: from effectiveness to greatness. New York: Free Express.

8. Helmick, C., and Swigger, K. (2006). Core competencies of library practitioners. Public Libraries, 45(2), 54-69.

9. Jagtap, Prashant and Kapade, Deepak (2011). Leadership: on the basis of values. IN Empowering Libraries for Life-long learning skills edited by Suresh Jange. Agra: Current Publications, 781-785.

10. Jordan, Mary Wilkins (2011). Developing Leadership Competencies in Librarians, IFLA 2011. Available at http:// conference.ifla.org/ifla77 (20th Apriul 2014).

11. Krishan Gopal (2006). Leadership in Academic Library of the Present Century. ILA Bulletin, 42 (3): 13-17

12. Mohan, A.Chandra. (2009). Leadership and Management: text, cases, Exercises. New Delhi: HPH.

13. Needham (2001). The concept of leadership in technology related organizations. Journal of Library Administration, 32 (3/4) :133-44.

14. Prakash, B and Patil, D B (2011). Leadership skills and change management in libraries. IN Empowering Libraries for Life-long learning skills edited by Suresh Jange. Agra: Current Publications, 762-766.

15. Ramesh Babu, B (2012). Leadership roles of librarians in the e-environment. IN EmpoweringLibraries for Life-long learning skills edited by Suresh Jange. Agra: Current Publications, 733-742

16. Rao, P.subba.(2013). Organization Behavior: Text, Cases & Games. New Delhi: HPH.

17. Stoglill, R.M(1974). Handbook of Leadership. New York: The Free Press.

18. Stueart, Robert D & Mortan, Barbara B.(2002). Library Information Center Management. Colord: Library Unlimited.

19. Tufts University, Development Guide for Tufts Leadership Competencies. *http://hr.tufts.edu/wpcontent/* uploads/ ODT_Leadership_Guide.pdf (25th March 2014).

20. Versosa, Fe Angela M. [2009]. Understanding library leadership: issues and concerns. Retrieved Oct. 7, 2009 from *http://www.slideshare.net/versosaaf/understanding-library-leaders-issuesandconcerns.*

21. Wang, Xuemao & Su, Chang (2006). Develop future library leaders with global in the context of cultural intelligence. Chinese Librarianship: an International Electronic Journal, 22. Available at: *http://www.white-clouds.com/icic/cliej/c/22wangsu.htm.*

22. Wikipedia (2009). Leadership. Retrieved on Oct. 6, 2009 from *http://en.wikipedia.org/wiki/leadership*

23. Winston, M. D., and L. Dunkley (2002). Leadership Competencies for Academic Librarians: The Importance of Development and Fund-Raising. College and Research Libraries 63(2): 171–182.

13

Assessment of Total Quality Management Practices in Academic Library and Information Services: An Empirical Study

Surendra Sethy*

ABSTRACT

Managing quality is one of the management challenges in libraries. Now a days, increasing expectations of users for better services have motivated libraries to view quality management as an effective means of incorporating quality improvement into their related services. Effectively implementing quality management in libraries requires an understanding of applying appropriate quality management concepts and techniques. This technique can be implemented and established in the day-to-day management of libraries successfully. A modern leadership style i.e the transformational leadership is required for the implementation of Quality Management in a library becoming an effective strategic goal.

* Assistant Librarian, Sir Padampat Singhania University, Udaipur, Rajasthan

Keywords : Total Quality Management, Quality, Quality principles, Academic Libraries, Information Services, TQM Barriers.

INTRODUCTION

The libraries have transformed drastically from storehouses for books and journals to the powerhouses of knowledge and information since the middle of the 20th century. The information and communication technology is responsible for this revolution. The very existences of libraries are dependable on users' satisfaction. Users are getting satisfied when the library is able to rise to his or her expectation or meet the actual needs. A quality service is said to be one, which satisfy the users' expectation resulting a good experience. Throughout the history, libraries were mainly concerned with collection development and processing. The library professionals gave less concern to quality in product and services never checked whether the users were satisfied or not. Gradually the social and economic changes have prompted the libraries to develop services. The staff has a vital role in the satisfaction of users. The library being a service organization, its prime objective is to provide the right documents, information and services to its users. Only the users' satisfaction survey will facilitate the assessment of their satisfaction with products and services offered. There are various methods, tools and techniques to measure, control and improve the quality of library services. Quality measurement and evaluation assumes great importance in modern libraries as it brings immense benefits to the library as well as user community. Libraries have always been committed to provide a high quality of services to its users. In the past, consuming more resources, buying more books, and moving to large premises are considered as improving quality. But that approach is not valid today. One of the good solutions to improve quality is to provide right information to a right user at right time. This requires a through change in the approach – an approach based on user requirements and user satisfaction. It is believed that this can be achieved by implementing TQM. Thus, TQM approach is slowly getting popular in today's libraries.

OBJECTIVES

The objectives of the present study are:

- To understand the concepts of Quality; Quality Management; and Total Quality Management;
- To present principles of TQM in the academic library and information service sectors;
- To examine the elements and application of TQM with regards to the services to academic library and information service sector;
- To examine the relationship between library science used in providing quality services;
- To know the benefits of TQM in academic library and information service sector used in providing quality services in the libraries;
- To present the best practice for implementation of TQM in libraries.
- To establish the barriers in the applicability of TQM in academic library and information service sector; and
- To suggest appropriate suggestions and conclusion to improve the TQM in academic library and information services for the betterment of the user

LITERATURE REVIEW

Following are some reviews of literature related to TQM.

The purpose of Begum Sayeda (2010) and others study was to explore the adoption of quality management practices in engineering educational institutions in India from management's perspective. The findings highlighted twenty seven critical factors/dimensions of quality management, which analyzed the relationship between TQM dimensions and institutional performance, which had been formulated using five dimensions. Positive and significant relationships among the TQM dimensions and institutional performance had been observed.

The purpose of Thakkar (2006) and other study was to explore the potential for adoption of TQM in self-financed technical institutions in the light of new demands and challenges posed by customers / students and society. The findings identified technical and students' requirements for the modern educational set-up. It provides information about the severity of various technical requirements of competitive education and recognized the need for continuous improvement, cultural change and effective use of financial resources to improve the value addition at each level.

The objective of Moghaddam & Moballeghi (2008) study was to present an overview of TQM in the library and information sectors. It was observed that TQM was initially applied as a management philosophy in the manufacturing sector. Following its enormous success, this philosophy was increasingly being applied in the service sector including libraries.

Pranjit (2007) has explained that Total Quality Management in libraries and information services has received considerable attention, with a majority of those investigations describing quality concepts, quality management principles, related processes, and limitations.

Fitech et al. (1993) pointed out that in today's competition; libraries have to provide quality services to its users, to validate their survival. So, now libraries are also started adopting TQM practices following other kinds of service industries

WHAT IS QUALITY?

Quality is an attribute of a product or service that fulfills or exceeds the human expectations. These expectations are based on the intended use and selling / service price. It is somewhat of an intangible based on perception. Quality has been defined variedly in different contexts. But one meaning of quality is customer satisfaction through product or by service. The customer in the academic library is user/reader/student. Here the customer is not outsider, but part of the academic community. Nunan and Calvert (1992) point out that: "The term quality defies any definition which will be universally accepted. When it is linked to performance, quality implies evaluation for comparative purpose; 'measures' of quality involve norms and standards and judgments of quality are assisted through use of norm or criterion referenced indicators. Where measurement focuses on the student as a product of education, quality is seen as education. When the emphasis is management of quality, attention focuses on strategies for achieving or improving quality."

According to Robinson, "quality is meeting the requirements of customer - now and in the future".

According to Sarkar, "quality of a product or service is the ability of the product or service to meet the users' requirements".

According to Juran and Gryna, define quality is "fitness for purpose".

According to Crosby, define quality as "conformance to requirement".

According to Deming, define quality as "uniformity with respect to correct target".

According to Weinberg, define quality as "value to some person".

The concepts of quality based definitions reveal two important dimensions i.e. customer satisfaction and continuous improvement. Consequently, we used a new definition of quality in terms of "customer focus".

In the context of the academic library and information service sector, it can be described as:

- Q - Quest for excellence of knowledge
- U - Understanding the user's need
- A - Actions to achieve user's demand
- L - Leadership quality for Librarian
- I - Involving all staff
- T - Team spirit in achieving common goals
- Y - Yardstick to measure progress

QUALITY PRINCIPLES

Following are the quality principles:

- Innovation in all areas including education and training
- Zero defect policy
- Quality prevention on line
- Reducing number of suppliers

- Use of statistical techniques to identify sources of waste
- Ensuring that the organizational and management support is for improving quality
- Continuous quality improvement
- Provide supervision with on line techniques
- Chart openness, do it together, teamwork is necessary
- Attack waste
- Designing products/services for quality so that products/services meet the requirements of the customers.
- Strategic quality planning, quality control and quality improvement system is needed.
- Everybody must be involved in quality improvement.
- Quality cannot afford weak processes
- Performance appraisal and reward system for employees is must for quality implementation.
- Measure and seek quality.

QUALITY MANAGEMENT

Customers are becoming the most important stakeholders. Libraries have adopted the most modern techniques of library administration with a purpose to give quality service to the users. Quality management as a concept provides comprehensive system to ensure quality, customer focus and continuous improvement in all organizations including academic library and information services. Brophy, Peter and Couling, Kate in their book 'Quality management and library science for information and library managers' says that quality is easy to recognize and difficult to define.

TOTAL QUALITY MANAGEMENT CONCEPTS

Total Quality Management is the art of managing the whole to achieve excellence. The golden rule is a simple but effective way to explain it. TQM is defined as both a philosophy and a set of guiding principles that represent the foundations of a continuously improving organization. It is the application of qualitative methods and human resources to improve all the processes within an organization and exceed customer needs now and in the future. TQM integrates fundamental management techniques, existing improvements, and technical tools under a disciplined approach (Talukder and Ghosh, 2004).

TQM is a concept created by W. Edwards Deming. It was originally introduced in Japan after world war-II to assist the Japanese in re-building their economy. The main focus of TQM is continuous quality improvements in the area of products, services, employer-employee relations and consumer business relations using the following 14 points:

- Create consistency of purpose for improvement of product and service;
- Adopt the new philosophy;
- Cease dependence on mass inspection to achieve quality;
- End the practice of awarding business on the basis of a price tag instead of minimizing total cost;
- Improve constantly and forever the system of production and service;
- Institute training for all employees;
- Adopt and institute leadership;
- Drive out of fear;
- Break down barriers between staff areas;
- Eliminate slogans, exhortations, and targets for the work force;
- Eliminate numerical quotas for the work force and eliminate numerical goals for people in management;
- Remove barriers that rob people of pride in their work;
- Encourage education and self-improvement for everyone;
- Take action to accomplish the transformation.
- According to British Standard BS 7850, TQM is defined as, "Management philosophy and company practices that aim to harness the human and material resources of an organization in the most effective way to achieve the objectives of the organization."

According to Jyotirmoy, "TQM is defined as conformance to requirement. TQM is a concept, the principles on which to develop a total quality culture, a journey that has no end and quality improvement is the enabling mechanism which must be continuous and companywide".

According to Oakland, "TQM is a systematic approach to the practice of management, requiring changes in organizational processes, strategic priorities, individual beliefs, individual attitudes and individual behaviours".

TQM is an enhancement to the traditional way of doing business. It is a proven technique to guarantee survival in world-class competition. Only by changing the actions of management will the culture and actions of an entire organization be transformed. TQM is for the most part common sense. Analyzing the three words, we have:

- **Total :** Everyone is involved in
- **Quality :** Continuously improving service to users
- **Management :** Act, art or manner of handling, controlling, directing etc.

Therefore, TQM is the art of managing the whole to achieve, excellence.

From the user's point of view, quality is an expression of the services usefulness in meeting the needs and expectations and its reliability, safety, durability and so on. One must plan their activities, implement the plan, and then check whether the plan is going accordingly or not. If there are any non-conformances with regard to quality and customer satisfaction, one must act immediately and take appropriate corrective and preventive action that is how quality standards are established on a continuous basis keeping in mind the overall long term holistic view of the total quality management (TQM).

TQM can be assessed by following bench making practice. It has five steps as explained below:

- Plan and select the activity
- Analyze the process
- Design the study and gather information
- Compare performance
- Design and implement improved activity.

TOTAL QUALITY MANAGEMENT PRINCIPLES

TQM is the application of a number of activities with perfect synergy. The philosophy of TQM is based on understanding customer needs and improving customer service and satisfaction. There are many elements of TQM addressed to different areas for change. The following are the most important elements of any total quality management (TQM) Programme:

- Customer-driven quality;
- Top management leadership and commitment;
- Continuous improvement;
- Fast response;
- Actions based on facts;
- Employee participation.

TQM culture (Crosby, 1979; Deming, 1986; Juran and Gryna, 1995).

IMPACTS OF RANGANATHAN'S FIVE LAWS IN QUALITY SERVICES

The fives laws of Rangnathan's help in quality improvement of services as those are concentrated to the user very seriously.

The First Law : "Books are for use" is a direction for measuring the quality of library. Quality in terms of contents, and availability as and when needed.

The Second Law : "Every reader his/her books" implies needs of readers.

The Third Law : "Every Book/information its reader" implies the importance of book selection in a library.

The Fourth Law : "Save the time of readers" indicate the importance of fast and efficient services to the users with the technologies.

The Fifth Law : "The library is growing organism "implies collection development, changing of all components of a library.

IMPLEMENTING QUALITY MANAGEMENT IN LIBRARIES AND INFORMATION SERVICES

Improvement in library services does not require any corporate environment, trainings, extra working hours etc. It can be achieved by using some management techniques like Total Quality engagement. TQM was initially applied as a management philosophy in the manufacturing sector. Following its massive success, this philosophy is being applied in the service sectors like banks, hospitals, insurance, academic institutions and in libraries too. Library is basically a service oriented organization. It provides services directly to the users or readers. Therefore, users' satisfaction is the primary or basic aim of every library and to provide better services for users' complete satisfaction, the utilization of library sources should be in adequate manner. Manpower or staff of the library is the key resources, so where as human being is involved the need of management techniques also will be there.

Basically a library has the following sections or cells: acquisition, circulation, technical, reference, online resources, audio-visual, reprographic, documentation etc. To carry out all the functions or activities of these sections efficiently, application of management techniques must be applied.

The practice of Quality Management in Library & Information Science sector existed since the evolution of the subject itself, but the terminology used for these varied widely. Performance indicators; performance evaluation; evaluation of reference sources using checklist of criteria; Evaluation of Information Retrieval systems using Precision and Recall rations; Cost-Benefit and cost effectiveness studies; user surveys depicting opinions on library services - all these studies make part and parcel of quality studies using different mechanisms of assessment and methodologies.

In early 1980s, numerous studies were made on automated data validation, error rates and patterns, authority control which belongs to quality control in online databases. However, customer and employee satisfaction are seldom in focus. Quality assurance studies were mostly restricted to special libraries and academic libraries. Although quality assurance studies based on

ISO 9000 and other accreditation schemes were conducted in libraries in UK, USA and Canada, such studies are rarely reported in Indian libraries and information systems.

The quality assurance initiative in LIS has primarily come from the parent organization to which it provides services. However, in the later years, the quality assurance system has become as essential feature of LIS management. Quality studies in LIS sector are mostly isolated and are made on different aspects of library management, services, user-studies, etc. The evidence produced by the few TQM cases in the LIS sector indicates that TQM is a highly relevant management theory for information sector.

Among the service industries such as Airlines, Banking institutions, Insurance companies and Health care providers, Libraries are the last to adopt TQM practices. For a long time, Librarians saw themselves as keepers of knowledge rather than active agents in information transfer. Though the main aim/ objective of libraries is to satisfy the users, the library professionals often forget that. But today libraries are pushed to a position where they have to provide quality services to its users, to justify their existence. So, now libraries are also started adopting TQM practices following other kinds of service industries.

Susan and Barnard present a model for the implementation of TQM in the library setting. It outlines a ten – step process divided into four stages shows as in fig. below. The approach is a flexible one that can be applied in different ways to a variety of situations depending on the level of support for implementing TQM both within and outside library.

Phase 1: The activities covered in phase one are quite useful to arrange a seminar exploring the implications of current technological developments and other societal changes that enhance the growth of the library community.

Phase 2 : Phase two emphasis on organizing quality once the commitment to TQM and structure is made. Quality / Service awareness, various aspects of library automation training should be given to all employees.

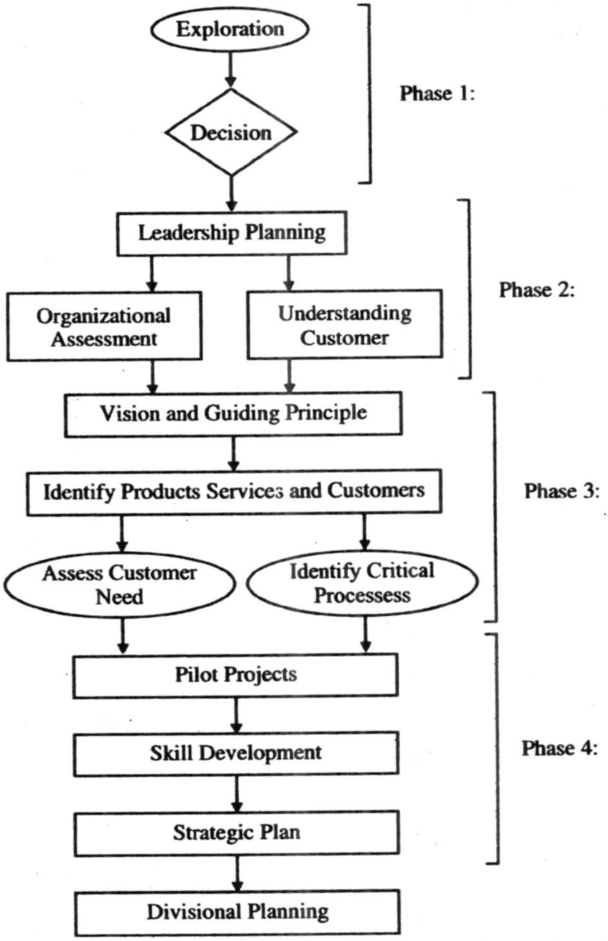

Fig. Implementation of TQM techniques in Library Services

Phase 3 : Phase three involves an extensive evaluation of current work processes and the relationship of these processes to customer needs and expectations. Laying heavy emphasis on team activity, team members will needs extensive training on the quality process including how customer judge services (e. g. reliability, responsiveness, assurance).

Phase 4 : In the process of expansion and integration, training can be extensive. Some employees even may need training even in new job skills as result of changed work processes particularly when a manual library is being converted into an automated library

BENEFITS OF TQM

What is attempted in the whole process of TQM is to introduce a new cultural change, through changing the style of people management which is likely to bring about greater participation from the employees who would work with management to achieve the organization goals and objective. TQM is a new concepts in management but it is equally beneficial to each and every organization like library. Dr. S.R. Ranganathan's fourth law of library science, 'Save the time of the readers' they have similar implications to what is advocated in TQM approach.

- Work itself becomes more interesting through greater involvement of employees.
- Increase in general productivity.
- Lower absenteeism because of greater job interest involvement of employees.
- All round greater team spirit. Improve and innovative process. By applying TQM technique, the librarians can not only satisfy the users consistently as per their needs and requirements but also improve quality of their services regularly.

In TQM Top management must convey to middle management that it believes TQM approach with the design of deliberate policy. Middle management is expected to conduct their affairs keeping TQM policy in view; conveying the decision to supervisors total quality management is a general philosophy of gradually improving the operations of a business through the application of accurate process analysis by every involved employee and business partner.Once the entire organization is geared to the change, the new culture would get engrained the organization leading to success. The more common approach to developing quality in libraries and information centers has been the adoption of Total Quality management.

CONCLUSION

Libraries are the ideal places to implement TQM. Libraries have to adopt new trends and techniques to provide best services to its users. The technological advancements during the last two decades have given a challenge to libraries to perform better in every situation. The users are very much aware about the new trends and are looking towards the librarians for getting them the right information at right time. TQM technique can help the libraries to make a good working system in which quality must be ensured in every department of the library. Many Libraries are following these practices in western countries and this trend is slowly coming to Asian countries and the countries like China and Singapore are the finest examples of using TQM techniques in Libraries. Every system requires time to be followed in the system. So libraries should try to follow TQM practices in their working and looking forward towards the positive changes occurred due to this in near future.

REFERENCES

1. Begum, S.S.N. (2003). Total quality management in the academic library. Library Philosophy and Practice. 5(2).
2. Fitch, D. K., Thomason, J. & Wells, E. C. (1993). Turning the library upside down: reorganization using total quality management principles, Journal of Academic Librarianship, Vol. 19 No. 5: 294-9.
3. Thakkar, J., Deshmukh, S. G. &Shastree, A. (2006). Total Quality Management (TQM) in self-financed technical intuitions: A quality function deployment (QFD) and force field analysis approach. Quality Assurance in Education, 14(1): 54-74.
4. Moghaddam, G., Golnessa&Moballeghi, M. (2008). Total quality management in library and information sectors. The Electronic Library, 26(6), 912-922.
5. Thakuria, Pranjit Kumar (2007). Concept of quality in library services: an overview. Planner, 412-420.
6. Hong Wang, (2006) From user to customer: TQM in academic libraries?. Library Management, Vol. 27 Iss: 9, pp.606 – 620
7. ErerjayaJayamalini, G. (1999), An overview of TQM in libraries. DRTC workshop on information management, 6-8 January
8. Nunan, T & Calvert, J (1995). Report of the project of Investigate

Quality and Standards in Distance Education.

9. Kanji, G.K. and Asher, M. (1993).Total Quality Management Process: a systematic approach, a supplement to Total Quality Management Vol.4

10. Brophy, Peter and Couling Kate. (1997) Quality management and library science: for information and library managers. Mumbai: Jaico Publishing House

11. Talukder, T. and Ghosh, S. (2004), Total quality management and its implication on library laws. SRELS Journal of Information Management, Vol. 41 No. 3, pp. 255-66.

12. Juran, J. M., Gryna, F. M.and Bingham, R. S. (Ed.). (1974). Quality Control Handbook. (3rd Ed.). New York: Mcgraw-Hill.

13. Susan Kumi and John Morrow (2006). Improving self service the six sigma way at Newcastle University Library Program: Electronic library and Information systems, Vol. 40, No. 2, pp 123-136.

14. http://www.ericdigests.org/1997-1/tqm.html

15. http://asq.org/learn-about-quality/total-quality-management/overview/deming-points.html

14

Massive Open Online Courses: A New Pedagogical Foundation to Online Learning

Satyam Prakash Tripathi*
Shriram Pandey**

ABSTRACT

The paper presents and outlook of Massive Open Online Courses (MOOCs) which are one of the latest trends in education, making it easier for learners to access free, high-quality learning opportunities around the world using World Wide Web. Paper explores conceptual framework supported by literature review and discusses MOOCs courses in general and more specially for LIS domain.

Keywords : MOOCs, LIS professional, e-learning

* Student M . Lib. I. Sc., Dept. of Library and Information Science Mohanlal Sukhadia University, Udaipur, Rajasthan, India.

** Asst. Professor & I/C, Mohanlal Sukhadia University, Udaipur, Rajasthan, India.

INTRODUCTION

Massive Open Online Course (MOOCs) are recent innovation is online/web based learning curves. It offers tremendous learning opportunities to a massive number of learners from anywhere in the world as long as they can access the course through internet. In general, a massive open online course (MOOC) is a free Web-based distance learning program that is designed for the participation of large numbers of geographically dispersed students.

The first MOOCs emerged from the open educational resources (OER) movement. The term MOOC was coined in 2008 by Dave Cormier of the University of Prince Edward Island in response to a course called connectivism and Connective Knowledge (Krantz, S. G., 2015).The original aim of MOOCs was to open up education and provide free access to university level education for as many students as possible. In contrast to traditional university online courses, MOOCs have two key features:

- **Open access :** anyone can participate in an online course for free
- **Scalability :** courses are designed to support an indefinite number of participants

However, these features may be interpreted differently by different MOOC providers; some MOOCs are massive but not open and some are open but not massive. By providing free online courses on demand, MOOCS enable learners to learn from anywhere irrespective of their situation as long as they have internet access.

The paper discusses MOOCs through a details literature review, followed by MOOCs courses and its applications to library and information science domain.

REVIEW OF LITERATURE

The review of literature on MOOCs has many dimensions and facets. Some of the important studies conducted on domain are briefly discussed as follows:

Xing W., et al., (2016) illustrates the effectiveness of an ensemble stacking generalization approach to build more robust and accurate prediction models than the direct application of base learners. Littlejohn A., et al., 2016 investigates the self-regulated learning (SRL) learners apply in a MOOC, in particular focusing on how learners' motivations for taking a MOOC influence their behavior and employment of SRL strategies. Macleod H., et al.(2016) concludes with a discussion of the potential opportunity for MOOCs to challenge standardization, homogenization and commodification of education. Shifting attention from the achievements of an individual to what can be done with a multitude; MOOCs may open up new educational arenas. Hood N., Littlejohn A. & Milligan C.(2015) examines how a learner's current role and context influences their ability to self-regulate their learning in a MOOC: Introduction to Data Science offered by Coursera. The study compared the self-reported self-regulated learning behaviour between learners from different contexts and with different roles. The study provides an insight into how an individual's context and role may impact their learning behaviour in MOOCs.Law P. (2015) discusses how the motivational aspects of digital badging support the growth in free, micro-credentialised courses against a backdrop of MOOC providers issuing certification for fee. The BOC project, which aligns with the University's Journeys from Informal to Formal Learning strategy, will help to provide accessible routes into the University for students who might not otherwise have the opportunity to participate and supports the OU Charter to promote the educational well-being of the community. Longstaff E.(2015) opines that collective aims of the three biggest providers of Massive Open Online Courses (MOOCs) are to promote anywhere, anytime learning; to increase access to world-class higher education; and to connect and empower . MOOCs can still be a beneficial education resource with an ability to empower even already well-educated members of society. Warburton S. &Mor Y. (2015) explores the design approaches that experts in the field of online learning have used to develop and deliver Massive Open Online Courses (MOOCs).Christo foraki M. & Ipeirotis P.G. (2015) discusses emergence of online labor platforms, online crowd sourcing sites, and even Massive Open Online Courses (MOOCs), has created an increasing need for reliably evaluating the skills of the participating users (e.g., "does a candidate know Java") in a scalable way. Many platforms already allow job candidates to take online tests to assess their competence in a variety of technical topics. Jones M.L.& Regner L. (2015) discuss two terms, student privacy and Massive Open Online Courses, have received a significant amount of attention recently. Both represent interesting sites of change in entrenched structures, one educational and one legal. MOOCs represent something college courses have never been able to provide: universal access .Mazzola L. 2015 discuss MOOCs as the combination of case study and personal reflection about developing and facilitating MoMA's first MOOC.

MOOC'S INITIATIVES

MOOC is increasingly gained popularity in recent years, and many of the reputed academic organizations around the world introduced MOOCs courses through different platforms. Some of the major initiatives are discussed in table 1.0 below.

Table 1. MOOCs Platform

Subject	Online Platforms
General works, Computer science and Information	Coursera, Computer Science | Free Online Courses
Philosophy and psychology	Philosophy and the Sciences (Coursera), Class Central, EIDYN
Religion	Coursera, course talk, Class Central
Social sciences	*Social Sciences | Free Online Courses ,course talk, Macquarie University*
Language	Languages & Literature, Stanford University, MOOCs for Learning Languages
Pure Science	Class Central, course talk, Quora, KDnuggets
Technology	Mooc list : Information, Technology, and Design, Massachusetts Institute of Technology, Coursera, ubiquity,
Arts & recreation	Class Central, course talk, Mooc list | Art, Coursera
Literature	Class Central, course talk, Literature | MOOC List, Open Yale Courses, Free Online literature courses

History & geography	Course talk, Quora, History | MOOC List, Geography | MOOC List, MOOCs - Springboard, Class Central, AHA.

MOOCs courses are being offered through various platforms and through different modes. A brief summary is given in Table 2.

Students from India being the second largest in terms of enrolment in MOOCS shows that their hunger for affordable and quality education and MOOCS are the best way to provide this to them. As a part of providing quality and affordable education to its students, Indian government has recently launched an Indian focused MOOC platform for all. This MOOC platform is termed as 'Swayam'- Study Webs of Active-learning for Young Aspiring Minds. Currently, SWAYAM is expected to offer three different courses - one from UC Berkeley's Umesh Vazarani's and two from IIT Bombay. And SWAYAM is going to use openEdx as its MOOC platform. Indian Institute of Management Bangalore has also joined edX and will host online course soon.

MOOCS FOR LIBRARY AND INFORMATION SCIENCE

There are many MOOCs available through WWW platform across world offred wide variety of courses across various disciplines. Some of the courses being offered through various platform are either deploy in practice for LIS domain or exclusively available for LIS domain are:

Butte College Library & Information Science: (http://www.butte.edu/services/library/learning/courses.html)

The Butte College Library is committed to providing quality information resources and services that meet the curriculum needs of our students. The Library also assists in fulfilling the diverse information needs of our entire college community and serves as an integral part in developing the skills used in lifelong learning. The library has a collection of over 70,000 print books, 70,000 eBooks, and 114,000 print and electronic periodicals. All the books and some of the electronic periodicals are searchable in our online catalog. A large reference collection, print magazines, journals, newspapers, and print books for checkout are housed.

Table 2. MOOCs Types

Provider	Type	Example Institutional Participant	Headquarter	Founded	Content License
WizIQ	Commercial	IIT Delhi, Des Moines Area Community College	India/USA	2007	Not Free, all rights reserved.
Stanford Online	Non-Profit	Stanford University	USA	2006	Free for registered users, personal/non-commercial usage
NPTEL	Non-profit	Indian Institutes of Technology, Indian Institute of Science	India	2006	Free, No registration, Creative Commons Attribution-Share Alike license
Mogul (website)	Commercial	N/A	USA	2015	Monthly subscription service.
Kadenze	Commercial	Stanford University, Princeton University, etc.	USA		
Coursera	Commercial	Stanford University, Princeton University, Arizona State University	USA	2012	Free for registered users, different course licenses
Khan Academy	Non-profit	N/A	USA	2006	Free, No registration needed, all rights reserved

Coursmos	Commercial	Stanford University, Draper University, MIT	USA	2014	-
Canvas Network	Commercial	Santa Clara University, University of Utah, Université Lille 1	USA	2008	All Rights Reserved, registration required.
Academic Earth	Non-profit	UC Berkeley, UCLA, University of Michigan, Oxford University	USA	2009	All rights reserved. Links to other courses with different licenses.
Future Learn	Non-profit	University of Birmingham, University of Edinburgh, etc.	UK	2012	All rights reserved

Idaho State Library ABLE (http://libraries.idaho.gov/page/able)

ABLE has been providing library basics for library staff world-wide since 1998. Over 5,000 ABLE Course Completion Certificates have been printed and distributed to individuals in 32 countries .

University of Wisconsin – Stout (http://www.uwstout.edu/soe/profdev/courses.cfm)

The UW-Stout School of Education offers challenging education programs that prepare highly qualified and successful teachers, leaders, and student services professionals. The mission of the School of Education is: "The School of Education (SOE) faculty and staff will engage in exemplary teaching, research, and service to ensure that graduates of the School become successful professional educators.

Info People (https://infopeople.org/)

Survival Spanish for Library Staff was an all-day workshop Info people developed to provide library staff with basic skills for communicating with Spanish-speaking patrons. Now the essential words and phrases taught in the workshop have been integrated into easy to digest MP3 files that are structured so that you can practice at your own pace, whenever you want, for as long as you want.

SJSU iSchool - San Jose State University / School of Information (http://ischool.sjsu.edu/programs/moocs)

The massive open online course (MOOC) program at the San José State University (SJSU) School of Information (school) brings individuals from diverse backgrounds and geographic regions together in an interactive online learning environment to explore the latest trends in the information profession. MOOC participants do not earn college credit. These open online courses are available to the public for free as professional development learning experiences. Please check back for upcoming MOOCs.

Alison http://alison.com/

ALISON is a 2.5 million-strong, global online learning community, filled with free, high-quality resources to help you develop essential, certified workplace skills. The mission at ALISON is simple: to enable you, wherever you are in the world, to learn and get certified new skills – at your own pace – using their free, interactive multimedia. There are hundreds of free courses to choose from, such as business & enterprise, languages, personal development and IT. ALISON is for anyone taking their first step towards a new or better job.T heir materials will help you to develop your creativity, confidence and competence for work, and to be as contented and productive as you can be in the world of work.

Coursera https://www.coursera.org/

Coursera believe in connecting people to a great education so that anyone around the world can learn without limits. Coursera is an education company that partners with the top universities and organizations in the world to offer courses online for anyone to take, for free. Their technology enables their partners to teach millions of students rather than hundreds. They envision a future where everyone has access to a world-class education that has so far been available to a select few. Classes offered on Coursera are designed to help you master the material. When you take one of their classes, you will watch lectures taught by world-class professors, learn at your own pace, test your knowledge, and reinforce concepts through interactive exercises. You'll also join a global community of thousands of students learning alongside you.

Open Learning https://www.openlearning.com/

Open Learning and their team from the University of New South Wales are happy to welcome all visitors, whether they are a student, teacher or someone in-between Students and teachers worldwide struggle to learn in an environment that focuses on delivering content with little room for community or creativity. Open Leaning's mission is to give you the freedom and the flexibility to form a community, express your creativity and discover yourself through education. The courses offer topics such as services marketing, programming and writing skills.

EduKart http://www.edukart.com/

EduKart.com is India's leading online education company that delivers high quality and industry relevant Online Distance Learning degree, international programs and certificate courses, so that working professionals and students pursuing higher education can easily learn relevant industry required skills and become a more valuable workforce.EduKart.com was started in 2011 by alumni of Stanford University, Indian Institute of Management (IIM) and University of Delhi. The founding team is immensely passionate about delivering high quality education and believe that EduKart.com creates a difference in the lives of those who aspire to move ahead. EduKart courses provide:

Udemy Free Courses https://www.udemy.com/

Udemy is an example of a site allows anyone to build or take online courses. Udemy's site exclaims, "Our goal is to disrupt and democratize education by enabling anyone to learn from the world's experts." The New York Times reported that Udemy, "recently announced a new Faculty Project, in which award-winning professors from universities like Dartmouth, the University of Virginia and North western offer free online courses. Its co-founder, Gagen Biyani, said the site has more than 100,000 students enrolled in its courses, including several, outside the Faculty Project, that charge fees." https://www. udemy.com/

CONCLUSIONS

It is clearly predictable that MOOCs has given a new pedagogy to online learning. MOOCs courses which are currently offered in various subject domains proved its relevancy and academic pursuance. There is certainly no doubt, that MOOCs has lots of potential to LIS domain and with quality content, best online lectures, great discussions, knowledgeable assessment quizzes, MOOCS will provide great opportunity to students to learn without fearing from failure. Therefore, it may be recommended to make use of Government initiatives like SWAYAM to develop MOOCs courses in LIS domain, especially in context of Indian Academic Scenario.

REFERENCES

1. Krantz, S. G. (2015). How to Teach Mathematics. American Mathematical Society.
2. Xing, W., Chen, X., Stein, J., &Marcinkowski, M. (2016). Temporal predication of dropouts in MOOCs: Reaching the low hanging fruit through stacking generalization. Computers in Human Behavior, 58, 119-129.
3. Littlejohn, A., Hood, N., Milligan, C., &Mustain, P. (2016). Learning in MOOCs: Motivations and self-regulated learning in MOOCs. The Internet and Higher Education, 29, 40-48
4. Macleod, H., Sinclair, C., Haywood, J., &Woodgate, A. (2015). Massive Open Online Courses: Designing for the unknown learner. Teaching in Higher Education, 21(1), 13-24.
5. Hood, N., Littlejohn, A., & Milligan, C. (2015). Context counts: How learners' contexts influence learning in a MOOC. Computers & Education, 91, 83-91.
6. Law, P. (2015). Digital badging at The Open University: Recognition for informal learning. Open Learning: The Journal of Open, Distance and E-Learning, 30(3), 221-234. (n.d.).
7. Longstaff, E. (2015). How MOOCs can empower learners: A comparison of provider goals and user experiences. Journal of Further and Higher Education,1-14. (n.d.).
8. Warburton, S., &Mor, Y. (2015). A set of patterns for the structured design of MOOCs. Open Learning: The Journal of Open, Distance and E-Learning, 30(3), 206-220. (n.d.).
9. Christoforaki, M., & Ipeirotis, P. G. (2015). A system for scalable and reliable technical-skill testing in online labor markets. Computer Networks, 90, 110-120. (n.d.).
10. Jones, M. L., &Regner, L. (2015). Users or Students? Privacy in University MOOCS. SciEng Ethics Science and Engineering Ethics. (n.d.).
11. Mazzola, L. (2015). MOOCs and Museums: Not Such Strange Bedfellows.Journal of Museum Education, 40(2), 159-170
12. Https://www.coursera.org/.
13. Https://www.class-central.com/subject/cs
14. Http://eidyn.ppls.ed.ac.uk/.
15. Https://www.coursetalk.com/.
16. Https://www.mq.edu.au/.
17. Http://www.stratford.edu/.

18. Http://www.kdnuggets.com/.

19. Https://www.quora.com/topic/Massive-Open-Online-Courses-MOOCs.

20. Http://www.ubiquityuniversity.org/.

21. Http://oyc.yale.edu/.

22. Https://www.springboard.com/blog/tag/moocs/.

23. Https://www.historians.orgHttps://en.wikipedia.org/wiki/Massive_open_online_course

24. Http://www.butte.edu/services/library/learning/courses.html.

25. Http://libraries.idaho.gov/page/ableHttp://www.uwstout.edu/soe/profdev/courses.cfm.

26. Https://infopeople.org/.

27. Http://ischool.sjsu.edu/programs/moocsHttp://alison.com/.

28. Https://www.openlearning.com/.

29. Https://www.openlearning.comHttp://www.edukart.com/.

30. Https://www.udemy.com/.

15

Collection Development Strategy in Library and Information Centers

Rabindra Kumar Mahapatra*
Surendra Sethy**

ABSTRACT

In libraries and information centers, collection development is considered an essential element of the information life cycle. The goal of any collection development organization must be to provide the library with a collection that meets the appropriate needs of its clients within the limits of its fiscal and personnel resources. To reach this goal, selection policies and practices play fundamental role in developing a strong collection. Collection development involves a number of activities by which a library acquires materials of all types by implementing the selection policy and the plans for document acquisition. Collection development is a dynamic and continuous activity. It involves the users, the library staff, and the subject experts on selection team. It is not an end in itself,

* Associate Professor, Dept. of Library and Information Science Tripura University, (Central University), Tripura.

** Asst. Librarian, Sir Padampat Singhania University, Udaipur, Rajasthan, India.

but a means to develop a need- based, up-to-date, and balanced collection fit to meet the document and information needs of the users.

Keyword : Library Collection, Library Resources, Collection Development strategy.

INTRODUCTION

Collection management is a set of interrelated activities involved in building and maintaining a collection of library resources to serve the needs and wants of its clients (Kennedy, 2006). The process of collection management includes evaluation of existing collections, making decisions about withdrawal, transfer and preservation. There are numerous challenges, trends and paradigm shifts occurring worldwide in collection development and collection management in libraries. Rapid development in ICT, information overload, changing trends in scholarly communication, diversion of funds; fiscal constraints are the major factors influencing the process of acquisition.

Library Services is committed to serving the information needs of the university through services and resources. This guide outlines the collection development procedures and responsibilities of library and departmental liaisons.

A library liaison is a professional librarian that works with departments to select materials for the collection; serves as a point of contact for questions regarding orders, collection development, account balances, and general library inquires; and shares information about library services.

A departmental liaison is a faculty member that submits orders on behalf of an academic unit, department, or division; and serves as the main point of contact to communicate the information and service needs of the department.

The term "collection development" refers to the process of systematically building library collections to serve study, teaching, research, recreational, and other needs of library users. The process includes selection and de-selection of current and retrospective materials, the planning of strategies for continuing acquisition, and evaluation of collections to determine how well they serve user needs.

Collection development is the means by which the library provides high quality information resources of print and non-print materials and provides access to electronic resources that will meet instructional requirements. Through collection development, we also strive to meet the cultural and recreational needs of the college community. Collection development is an ongoing process, undertaken by librarians and library services staff, with input from faculty, administrators, staff, and students.

Now a day's Librarians working in 21st Century in academic libraries are vested with the responsibility to build and shape collections that not only demonstrate contemporary relevance, but are sufficiently responsive to the information needs of tomorrow's user.

The purpose of the Collection Development statement is to describe the library's collections and collecting efforts in terms of their organization and scope, the various types of publications and materials collected, and the methods and procedures deemed most useful and efficient in collection development efforts.

LIBRARY COLLECTION

Libraries were the first formed in response to the objective need of human society to accumulate, preserve, and disseminate the information contained in written works. In modern times, each country's library collections taken as a whole represent the wealth of the country and serve as an indicator of the national level of education and culture.

There are three types of library collections i.e. general, subject, and specialized and these are divided into such categories as books, journals, newspapers, audiovisual materials, pictorial publications, sheet music, phonograph records, maps, and microfilms, depending upon the nature of the collection.

"Library collection is a sum of library materials books, manuscripts, serials, pamphlets, reports, recording, microfilm, e-resources and online resources etc. that make up the holdings of a particular library".

COLLECTION DEVELOPMENT

Library collection development is the process of meeting the information needs of the people (a service population) in a timely and economical manner using information resources locally held, as well as from other organizations.

According to The International Federation of Library Associations and Institutions (IFLA), acquisition and collection development focuses on methodological and topical themes pertaining to acquisition of print and other analogue library materials (by purchase, exchange, gift, legal deposit), and the licensing and purchase of electronic information resources,

Collection development is a most important process of library. In which increase the reading materials of library for satisfaction of reader approach.

- A set of resources that will be most useful for community.
- In recent time the term "collection development" has come to encompass a broad range of activities related to the policies and procedures of selection, acquisition and evaluation of library collection

STRATEGY FOR COLLECTION DEVELOPMENT

Collection development is considered as one of the primary tasks for any library and information Centre. It is a dynamic and continuous activity. In order to develop a balanced, user-oriented and active collection, a well planned and thought out system has to be evolved by the library and information managers in close association with the representatives of various user constituencies. Such a system will not only help develop need based collection but also save money, time and space that would, otherwise, be wasted on developing irrelevant, outdated, and passive collections.

Some of the strategies involved in collection development at Library are:-

1. Analysis of the information needs of the users;
2. Formulation and implementation of selection policy to suit the objectives of the library;
3. Acquisition programmes to build-up a balanced

collection;

4. Resource sharing and its impact on collection development;
5. Weeding out programmes to ensure effectiveness of collection;
6. Competitive vendors profile and rational budget; and
7. Collection evaluation

COLLECTION DEVELOPMENT GUIDELINES

There are some certain general criteria for selecting resources for the library and they are followings:

- All Resources, regardless of formats, are selected according to the general criteria. Resources selected may be in wide range of formats, including print, electronic and audio-visual formats.
- Where a choice must be made between different formats for the same material, consideration is given to cost, ownership or access, anticipated level of use, availability in preferred format, and space requirements .
- Resources should be relevant to the teaching, research and scholarship at the university and support the institution's strategic and cultural priorities.
- Subject content should be at an appropriate academic level.
- The quality of research and the accuracy and currency of the content of any new resource should be verified.
- New resources should balance the collection or fill identified gaps in the collection.
- Flexibility to develop collections for new programmes and to expand existing collections to meet curriculum changes should be maintained.
- Since most of the University Library resources are purchased in foreign currency, decisions to purchase are influenced by the ongoing fluctuations in the exchange rates.
- While mindful that we live in a multi-lingual society,

preference is given to English language works, except for materials needed for the study of other languages and literatures taught at the University.

- Duplication of any resource should be avoided, except in certain circumstances listed in the policy on duplication.

(Duplicates are not normally purchased and not encouraged due to budget and space considerations. The Library recognizes that duplicate copies may be needed to meet special teaching and learning requirements and provides the following criteria for their purchase:

- Heavy and continuous usage,
- No more than 5 copies will be purchased and the number of copies will be dependent on student numbers requiring use of the title
- Requests will require supporting justification and must be approved by the relevant HOD and library management committee.)

PRE-REQUISITES OF COLLECTION DEVELOPMENT

- We should be known specific objectives for library.
- Librarian should be created a CDP.
- Librarian should be kept a balance between need of readers and objective of library.
- Librarian should be established a book selection committee.
- All the rules should be followed by librarian for best library collection.

COLLECTION DEVELOPMENT POLICY

A policy which is created for the developing of library collection in which include Identification, selection, acquisition and evaluation of reading materials called as a Collection Development.

Collection development policy establishes ground rules for planning budgeting, selecting and acquiring library materials. These documents provide a framework for coordinated collection development programme throughout libraries.

Collection development policies also function as a guide to library resources for faculty, other users and other libraries by describing the scope and nature of the collection.

The development and implementation of a collection development policy is a best practices for libraries and it includes the following task:

Define the objectives of your library : State clearly the purpose of its existence.

Define your user community and their information needs : This requires complete knowledge and understanding about library stakeholders. This may include adult education teams, extension workers and adult education professionals, local community members and those who provide funds for the library. Their information needs can be accessed through library surveys, personal interviews, and informal discussions with all stakeholders.

Define library policy for building collections : The policy states the guiding principles and procedures under which collection development activities, including the selection, maintenance, and weeding of print, electronic, and media library materials will occur. This would also mean specifying subject areas of interest to library stakeholders, their languages preferences, and formats of published and unpublished material (i.e. print, non-print, or electronic format). Non-print material could include films, slides, transparencies, photographs, maps posters, charts, etc. The policy must also define the limits in terms of collection size, keeping in view the users strength in a given subject, space available within the library premises, and annual budget earmarked for the purpose. The policy may also specify the subject areas in which the library is going build its archival collection, if any. Such a policy statement on the part of the library ensures continuity and consistency in selection and revision of materials for the library collections.

Define what different collections are required to be developed and sustained keeping in view users' information needs : The possible options include books collection, reports collection, pamphlet collection, multimedia collection, and reference collection (comprising dictionaries, yearbooks, directories, who's who almanacs, general and subject encyclopedias), etc. The library may decide on developing some of these collections keeping in view the users' information needs.

Define your book selection policy : State the distribution of library budget by subject and by collection. The policy may also state guidelines for acquiring multiple copies of books, guidelines for accepting books from donors, and guidelines for weeding out material

Weeding is an important but difficult aspect of collection development in a library. A librarian may withdraw materials based on the condition, age, relevancy, or lack of space for an item.

CRITERIA FOR COLLECTION DEVELOPMENT

The Library collects materials in formats best suited to the user and the content. The same criteria are used to select print, audiovisual or electronic materials. The needs of users are considered in the selection process.

Materials in electronic formats are preferred when they meet several of the Following criteria

- Easy to use
- Easy to Access
- Available through remote access
- Board coverage
- Full text content
- Content Suitable to format
- Reliable vendor
- Reasonable cost

SCOPE OF THE COLLECTION DEVELOPMENT

The Library collection holds resources designed to support the learning, teaching and research needs of the University. Resources are provided in a variety of formats including:

- Books and other hard-copy printed materials
- Serials (i.e. journals, periodicals or newspapers in both electronic or hard-copy format)

- Databases (electronic collections containing bibliographic citations and/or full-text items)
- Multimedia material (including CDs, DVDs, computer software, and online) etc

MAJOR ELEMENTS OF CDP

Purpose of Collection Development : The acquisition and maintenance of the library's materials collection is a primary function of the library's mission. Collection development refers to the process of building and maintaining the library's entire materials collection, in both print and non-print formats. The Purpose of Collection Development Selecting best and useful documents for readers. The development and maintenance of library collections is a joint responsibility of faculty and the professional staff of the library.

Gifts and Donations : Any gifts donated to the library become the property of the library, and will not be returned to the donors. Textbooks and other study materials donated by faculties and students are welcome as gifts.

Some other elements of collection development policy are such as patrons, Materials, Selectors, selection methods and tools, Acquisition, Physical space, copy right policy etc.

ADVANTAGE OF CDP

- It helps to giving a base for accurate planning of collection development.
- It helps in best selection and acquisition of books and other reading materials.
- It helps to appropriate use of money for purchasing books and other reading material.
- It helps in weeding out the waste reading material.
- It helps in fulfill first, second and third law of Library science.

Processes of Collection Development : Collection development is a process of maintaining balanced consistence and user responsive collection in the library. There are some certain collection development processes which are given below:

- Decide objectives of collection development.
- Create a CDP in written.
- Make a selection committee.
- Select reading materials according to different criteria and features.
- Take a sanction of selected reading materials from library authority.
- Select distributor or vendor and commit to ordering, delivery and receiving process.
- Coordinate selected reading materials with available budget.
- Make a list and ordering of selected reading materials.
- Receive and check ordered material.
- Replace damage reading material.
- Reminder to distributor or vendor.
- Physical process of reading materials.
- Shelving of reading materials.
- CREW (Continuous Review, Evaluation and Weeding)

Techniques of Collection Development : The techniques of collection development which are include:

- User survey, general meeting and interview to knowing their approaches.
- Read recent book reviews.
- Motivate to community for giving donation and gift on special occasion.
- Replace the waste reading material with other libraries.
- Through Inter library loan and resource sharing.
- If your library is part of a larger organization request permission from your funding agency.
- Invite and display library services in front of officers who support financially for collection development.

EVALUATION OF COLLECTION DEVELOPMENT

- According to objectives of collection development.

- According to Users approaches.
- Updating of collection
- Proper forms of reading material.
- Authenticity of reading material.
- Use of collection
- Physical conditions of reading material

CONCLUSION

In today's electronic environment, collection development is becoming collection management, which is much wider in scope. The librarian must act as a knowledge manager, applying the skills right from collection planning, selection, analysis and cooperation in order to manage the intersection of both print and e-resources. They need to think about the availability and accessibility of multiple electronic formats in order to deliver the best information to all users in the least possible time. The web has introduced new resources to collection managers throughout the world.

REFERENCE

1. Kenedy, John. (2006). Collection management: A concise introduction (rev. ed.). WaggaWagga,NSW: Centre for Information Studies, Charles Sturt University.
2. https://en.wikipedia.org
3. https://www.ohio.edu/lancaster/academicsupport/library/upload/Collection-Development-2015.pdf
4. Hoffman,F.W.&Wood,R.J.(2005).LibraryCollectionDevelopment Policies:Academic,Public,andSpecialLibraries.Toronto: ScarecrowPress.
5. Mahapatra, Piyush Kanti (2000). Collection Management in Libraries, EES Publications, New Delhi. Pp 15.
6. www.google.com

16

Knowledge Management in Libraries

P. K. Panigrahi*

ABSTRACT

The term "Knowledge Management" was started and popularized in the business world during the last decade of the 20th century. The business world first recognizes the importance of knowledge in the "global economy" of the "knowledge age". Knowledge management is concerned with the process of identifying; acquiring, distributing and maintaining knowledge to improve an organization's performance. In the present age of information communication technology both information and knowledge have become essential ingredients due to multi-dimensional use and application in the society. They have also been playing an important role to change and improve the current society for future vision.

The knowledge management (KM) has become an important guideline for the Information and Knowledge Society, as well as for libraries. The successful implementation of KM is that people will share what they know and reuse the expertise of others. Development of information technology (IT) and its

* Librarian, Sir Padampat Singhania University, Udaipur, Rajasthan

applications in Library and Information Centers, the concept of document management has been changed to information management and again the entire scenario of information management has started its change to knowledge management. This article approaches the process of knowledge management which can help libraries to better adapt to the new requirements of the digital age and meet users' needs. This paper also describes the development and use of information and communication technologies (ICT) in the library and information centers.

Keywords : Knowledge Management, Knowledge age, Data, Information, Information Management, Tacit Knowledge, Explicit Knowledge, OPAC, Decision making.

INTRODUCTION

The term "Knowledge Management" was started and popularized in the business world during the last decade of the 20th century. The business world first recognizes the importance of knowledge in the "global economy" of the "knowledge age". Knowledge management is concerned with the process of identifying; acquiring, distributing and maintaining knowledge to improve an organization's performance.

In the present age of information communication technology both information and knowledge have become essential ingredients due to multi-dimensional use and application in the society. They have also been playing an important role to change and improve the current society for future vision.

The advent of the internet and related technological developments has transformed the nature of library and information centres. In library and information science, Ranganathan (2011) was the first to advocate that a universe of subjects is synonymous to a universe of knowledge and therefore proposed the concept of knowledge management in libraries. To prove their relevance and value the libraries must strive to provide the right amount of information to the right clientele at the right time with a right expense of financial and human resources. Library & Information centres needs to apply knowledge management practices to support provide better results. A library's status is earlier defined by the collection it housed; it is extended to include online and seamless access to information resources.

KM SYSTEMS TODAY

Knowledge Management has reached a turning point in its evolution. Companies, convinced of the inherent business value, are now focusing on the dual problems of how to successfully implement KM, and how to choose from the bewildering array of solutions offered by consultants and vendors alike, many of whom have made the 'easy' transition from being data management companies to being 'knowledge' companies. So with the wide array of solutions available today, how come knowledge management efforts still fail so often? Although many reasons have been postulated, few are as important as making sure that you understand how knowledge is used and created in your organization, and making sure that you have a balanced knowledge system portfolio that not only captures, stores, and disseminates your corporate knowledge, but also allows opportunity for the creation of knowledge.

Why do current Knowledge Management (KM) systems find it so hard to achieve solid Return-On-Investment (ROI)? And why is it that so many KM success stories revolve around the impromptu, unofficial applications of technology by informal Communities of Practice? In order to take a fully balanced approach to building a comprehensive and successful KM system, you have to take several factors into account. What is the knowledge that you're trying to collect? What form is it in? What are you trying to do with the knowledge?

When are you planning to use it? How are you planning to use it? These are all questions that are frequently forgotten by the KM practitioner – and by most KM vendors who, for the sake of simplicity, generally push a one-size fits all approach to KM. Unfortunately, these tend to be very one-sided solutions as KM vendors tend to ignore the harder elements of KM in favor of the elements that their software can do well – that of data collection, storage, and manipulation. However, it is well documented by many influential KM thought leaders that it is the human side of the equation that has the biggest potential for yielding the solid results that executives are looking for from KM systems.

In fact, KM has long been plagued by its inability to show unambiguous metrics that can demonstrate a solid monetary return to boardroom executives without using assumptions that generally range from the subjective to pure fantasy. This is not to say that benefits don't accrue – but the reality is that the vast majority of 'traditional' KM systems and programs revolve around the achievement of intangible benefits. Whilst those benefits can make all the difference between winning and losing in the knowledge economy, the purse string holders still want to see visible results of their money being well spent.

The benefit of the human element can best be seen by looking at KM systems and processes which revolve around the seemingly fabled entities that are "Communities of Practice". Communities of Practice (CoPs) are informal groups of practitioners, experts, and other interested parties who trust each other to provide relevant and accurate knowledge as and when needed. KM experts and IT vendors have been quick to jump on this concept and a huge industry has been built around trying to artificially create CoPs, formalize them, or else support these groups and individual practitioners through the use of knowledge repositories and other KM tools. The two approaches are different in many ways – and it has become hard for companies to fully understand what they are dealing with because more often than not the two approaches come under the same over-reaching label: Knowledge Management. As a result, companies choose one or another and find themselves missing half the equation of what is in reality a symbiotic relationship between the main types. Let's take a closer look.

CHARACTERISTICS OF KM

Information and knowledge are vast and just like something "ocean; as ocean is categories in differently, as geographically, economically, and scientifically and are in many other forms. It may be applicable into different sector for valuable recreation.

The characteristic of KM are indicated as follows:

- KM is about people
- KM is orderly & goal directed
- Knowledge is ever changing
- KM is value added
- KM is visionary
- KM. is complementary

These can be subdivided into the following:

Recognize the role of information Management in creating value : An organization must recognize and accept the critical role of Information Management. It plays in the success of an organization and the leadership role. The CIO must assume in order to maximize the full potential of Information Technology.

Position of the CIO for success : The CIO must be recognized as a full participant of the Executive Management in team and will be given the technical and Management skills.

To meet business need.

International firm activity and innovation : Using a knowledge production framework and a rich set of plan level data.

KM is visionary : This vision is expressed is strategic business term rather than technical terms and in a manner which generates enthusiasm by motivation for managers to work together towards the reaching common goals.

WHAT IS KNOWLEDGE MANAGEMENT?

In a preliminary way, let it suggests that knowledge management is the systematic:

- underpinning
- observation
- instrumentation
- and optimization
- of the firm's knowledge economies.

These activities – or perhaps process areas – are sequential. That is to say, it is not possible to optimize a firm's knowledge economies until they are instrumented; instrumentation is selective measurement based on empirical observation and observation of the for-the-most-part underground knowledge economies within the firm requires that these economies be brought out into the light of day, made official, and formally underpinned with technology, process and policy that makes construction, embodiment, dissemination and use of knowledge officially-sanctioned and formally-valued activities within the firm. This definition suggests what knowledge management might be, or more precisely what people who call themselves knowledge managers might do. What it does not provide is:

- any clear sense of what objectives knowledge managers have in view when they begin the process of underpinning, observing, incrementing and optimizing their firm's knowledge economies.
- any formal definition of the limits to effective knowledge management within each phase, the dangers inherent in the tasks at hand, or the complexities associated with design and implementation decisions and trade-offs.

The first problem – lack of a clear sense of objectives – is resolved, at least conceptually, with ease: all knowledge management programs ought to be targeted directly at the firm's income statement: at revenue enhancement, cost reduction, or the management of risk associated with market place and financial performance. In practice, this is a difficult task, implying a thorough understanding of the firm's internal value chain and the value systems in which it participates, and further implying a formal understanding, at a strategic level within the firm, of the role knowledge plays in the firm's quest to add value. Ultimately, all knowledge management programs and problems are local: unique to a particular.

DATA, INFORMATION AND KNOWLEDGE

Data, Information and knowledge are three steps through which a Knowledge Management (KM) system grows. Besides these, there are two more steps, which are invariable associated with KM - understanding and wisdom. The latter two require more human intervention.

- **Data** is raw. It does not convey any meaning. It simply exists without any significance and usability. Data are collected from a study involving observation, experimentations & surveys.
- **Information** is data that has been given meaning attaching context to it by way of relational connection.

  Marc Porat states that "Information is data that has been organized and communicated".Stehen Abram sees the process for knowledge creation and use as a continuum where data transforms into information, information transforms into knowledge and knowledge drives and undergoing behaviour and decision making.
- **Knowledge** is storage of information, which can be recalled for decision-making. Knowledge in some instances is nothing but memorization. It does not provide power of inference and reasoning so that new knowledge can be generated. According to Denham grey, Knowledge is the full utilization of information and data, coupled with the potential of people's skills, competencies, ideas, intuitions, commitments, talents, root causes, relationships, perspectives and concepts.
- **Understanding** means learning while knowledge is just memorizing something. It is cognitive and analytical.
- **Wisdom** is the process by which one can judge between right and wrong, good and bad. Wisdom is a uniquely human state.

The following diagram represents the transitions from data, to information, to knowledge, and finally to wisdom, and it is understanding that supports the transition from each stage to the next. Understanding is not a separate level of its own.

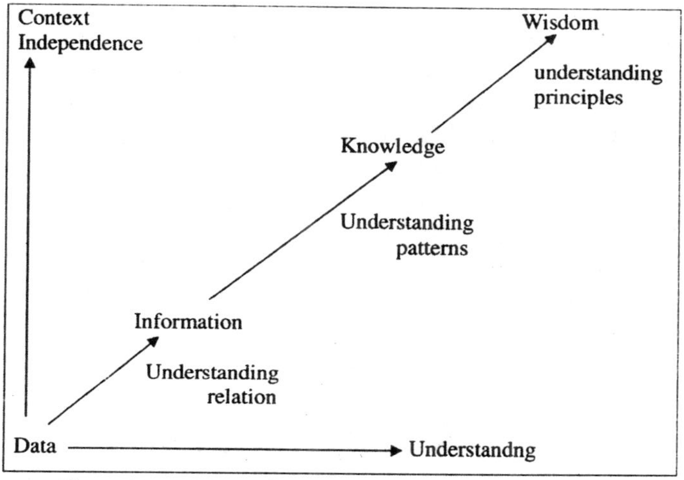

Fig. 1. Transition of Data, Information, Knowledge

TYPES OF KNOWLEDGE

Knowledge can be classified in two broad categories: tacit and explicit.

Tacit Knowledge : Tacit knowledge is subjective and experience based knowledge that cannot be expressed in words, sentences, numbers or formulas, often because it is context specific. It resides in the human mind. So it is hard to formalize, often even difficult to communicate. This type of knowledge can be seen in the behaviour or action of a person.

The basic problem is that tacit knowledge is rarely recorded and shared in business organizations even though tacit knowledge may be the real key getting things done.

Explicit Knowledge : Explicit knowledge is objective and rational knowledge that can be expressed in words, sentences, numbers or formulas (context free). It includes theoretical approaches, problem solving manuals and databases. It is well communicable and available in media.

KNOWLEDGE MANAGEMENT (KM)

The Knowledge available in the human mind is difficult to access and on the other hand the knowledge available in books or in other media is easily accessible. Knowledge management is concerned with the exploitation and development of the knowledge assets of an organization with a view to furthering the organization's objectives. The knowledge to be managed includes both explicit, documented knowledge, and tacit, subjective knowledge. Management entails all of those processes associated with the identification, sharing and creation of knowledge. This requires systems for the creation and maintenance of knowledge repositories, and to cultivate and facilitate the sharing of knowledge and organizational learning. Organizations that succeed in knowledge management are likely to view knowledge as an asset and to develop organizational norms and values, which support the creation and sharing of knowledge.

DEFINITION OF KNOWLEDGE MANAGEMENT

There are several definitions for Knowledge Management. Given below, are some of the most commonly used definitions:

De Jarnett

Powerful environmental forces are reshaping the world of the manager of the 21st century. These forces call for a fundamental shift in organization process and HR strategy. This is knowledge management.

Taylor

Knowledge management is the process of critically managing knowledge to meet existing needs, to identify and exploit existing and acquired knowledge assets and to develop new opportunities.

Peters

Knowledge management is the activity, which is concerned with strategy and tactics to manage human cantered assets.

Brooking

Knowledge management is about enhancing the use of organizational knowledge through sound practices of information management and organizational learning.

VALUE OF KNOWLEDGE MANAGEMENT

In an organizational context, data represents facts or values of results, and relations between data and its context have the capacity to represent information. Knowledge Management enables the members of the organization to deal with today's situations and effectively create their future. If a particular situation is already addressed by someone and that is recorded, the same can be applied whenever similar situations arise, which avoids duplication of work.

NEED FOR KNOWLEDGE MANAGEMENT

The need of knowledge management is to find effective ways to translate the organisation's on going experience into knowledge. It transferring and leveraging organizations and institutions knowledge across time and space. For this the following issues can be taken care;

Sharing of information : Research organizations and business organizations require heavy sharing of knowledge, because they are productive.

Decision Making : Another need of KM is decision making or policy making. KM acts as tool for the policy makers of an organization, which assists them to take serious policy decision or day to day decisions. This is because it has knowledge base, which contains the decision on the same or related situations.

Access to information : KM provides access to information required by any of corporate bodies, executive or research oriented. It helps them to find the answer of their questions or assists them in finding the answer.

Economy : KM helps in saving resources through the proper communication among the researchers and executives. KM provides the knowledge within the organization or if needed outside the organization. So, it avoids duplication of work.

TECHNOLOGY AND KNOWLEDGE MANAGEMENT

The concept of KM would be less powerful for organisations without knowledge oriented technologies. Technology's important role in KM is extending the speed of knowledge transfer. Knowledge engineering, digital networks, the internet and intranets are not KM but only enabling technology for managing knowledge. KM technology enables users to simultaneously access internet sites, databases, intranets and other internal/external resources as if the information existed in a single location. Improved collaborative technologies enhance person-to-person communication, thus helping in the development of knowledge across organisational and geographical boundaries. The following diagram reflects the main technologies that support knowledge management.

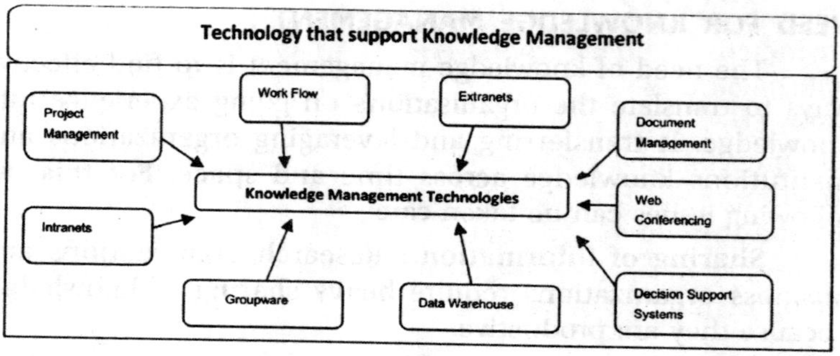

Fig. 2. Technology that support knowledge management

ROLE OF LIBRARIES IN KNOWLEDGE MANAGEMENT

Now days, Libraries should improve their knowledge management in all of the key areas of library services. The new role of libraries in the 21st century needs to be as a learning and knowledge centre for their users. As a learning organization, libraries should provide a strong leadership in knowledge management. To cope with the exponential growth in human knowledge, libraries need to develop their resources, access and sharing strategies from printed to electronic and digital resources. Limited by funding, technology, staff and space, libraries must carefully analyse the needs of their users and seek to develop cooperative acquisition plans to meet the needs of users. Libraries should be developed and maintained an integrated online public access catalogue (OPAC) with both internal and external resources as well as printed and other formats of knowledge. Useful websites and knowledge sources should be regularly searched and selected from the internet and included in OPACs. In the current digital and networked knowledge age, the size of information sources on the web is growing exponentially. No one really knows exactly how many web pages are on the internet, because new web pages are added every second. Universities and research organizations are acknowledged the reservoirs. These highly valued intellectual assets, regardless of whether they are explicit or tacit, should be inventoried, archived, indexed, frequently updated and made accessible in digital form. Libraries should use the new approach to capture web information by cooperative efforts such as Dublin core metadata and the Cooperative Online Resources Catalogue (CORC). Other new methods such as data mining, text mining, content management, search engines, natural language searching, linguistic analysis, semantic networks, knowledge extraction, concept of yellow pages and such technologies in information visualization as two dimensional or three dimensional knowledge mapping etc., have been a part of recent developments in knowledge management systems.

ROLE OF LIBRARIAN IN KNOWLEDGE MANAGEMENT

Knowledge Management team is not a one-man show. There are many components of KM. These components belong to all the areas of the organization. The job of Librarian is to provide right information to the right person at the right time. Thus, they are an unavoidable element of the knowledge management team. The following are some of the important activities of the librarian on knowledge management.

Knowledge Maps : This involves constructing an actual map of a special database, which points to where the resources are available. Using the knowledge map it is possible to contact the resource person or access the required data.

Acquisitions : The collection building should be extended to knowledge available inside the organization. The Librarian works with the knowledge team to survey the various in-house documents, to identify and digitize those of archival and retrieval value. Technical organizations have a substantial collection of this kind-drawings, standards, reports and records of technical discussions.

Categorising : The knowledge located, inside or outside, has to be represented in a manner suitable for access or transfer. For this purpose, it has to categorize in hierarchical schemes based on a controlled vocabulary. Obviously the librarian is the most suitable professional for this task. An additional task is that of coordinating and linking the various pieces of knowledge gathered by the respective technical departments, called knowledge communities.

Narratives : This involves extracting success stories and technical anecdotes from resource person and diffusing them over a corporate network. Surprisingly this age old mode of dissemination has proved quite effective in certain companies.

Capturing Tacit knowledge : It might be seen that the most difficult codification task pertains to tacit knowledge, as it is personal expertise built over the years, which cannot adequately be expressed in words. The traditional method of apprenticing juniors to veterans, so as to transfer their expertise before retirement, still holds good. DVD making or online storing of conversation and actions of technical veterans is a possibility.

Managing Databases : It is said that, for the tasks of maintaining the intranet, managing new inputs, user access control, etc, which can be viewed as extensions of circulation control, acquisition, etc., the librarian is a good choice.

CONCLUSIONS

Knowledge Management requires to be accepted as a key factor of the overall business strategy. Library may play an important role in success of knowledge management for their organization. Libraries take care of tacit knowledge in a better way for their successful working and satisfy their users.The library and Information professionals are best knowledge creators. Information technology and systems can provide effective support in implementing knowledge management. Librarians should train themselves and their staff to develop the appropriate knowledge management systems and use information technologies to equipped libraries to provide better, faster and pinpointed services to its users. The librarian's roles should not be limited to being the custodians of information but they have to acquire skills to keep themselves updated so as to cope intelligently and objectively with the effective and efficient knowledge management in the libraries. Library professionals have to recast their roles as knowledge professional.

REFERENCES

1. Albert, S. (1998).Knowledge Management: Living Up To The Hype? Midrange systems, 11(13), pp.52.
2. Anthes, G.H. (1991).A Step Beyond a Database. Computerworld, 25(9), pp. 28.
3. Applegate, L., Cash, J. & Mills D.Q. (1988). Information Technology and Tomorrow's Manager. In McGowan, W.G. (Ed.). Revolution in Real Time: Managing Information Technology in the 1990s, pp. 33-48, Boston, MA, Harvard Business School Press.
4. Hwa-WeiLee(2005) . Knowledge Management and the Role of Libraries.published on the 3rd China-US Library Conference.
5. Ranganathan, S. R. (2011).Five laws of librarianship. In Wikipedia the Free Encyclopedia. Available online at http://en.wikipedia.org/wiki/Five_laws_of_library_science. Accessed February 24, 2011.
6. Raja, Md.Wasim., Ahmed, Md. Zudair., &Sinha, Arun K. (2009).Knowledge Management and Academic Libraries in IT Era. ICAL Poster Papers.
7. Saha, Tannmay (2015). Application of Knowledge Management in Modern Academic Libraries. International Journal of Arts, Humanities and Management Studies, 1(7), pp.27-34.
8. Kumar, Sunil & Mishra, Bhawna (2012). Knowledge Management: Important Tool for the success of an organization. International Journal of Management Research & Review, 2(5), pp.697-701
9. Husain, S. & Nazim, M. (2013). Concepts of knowledge management among library &information science professionals. International Journal of Information Dissemination and Technology, 3(4), pp.264-269
10. Bansal, Alka (2000). Knowledge Management: A Review. DESIDOC Bulletin of Information Technology, 20(4), pp.3-9.
11. Madaan, Deepti (2007). Knowledge Management in Libraries: Gaining Competitive Advantage through E- Learning. 5th International CALIBER, Panjab University, Chandigarh, 08-10 February, 2007, pp.283-294.

